"Lots of marvelous information to jazz up your next speech."
— Pat McNees, speechwriter and author of
YPO: The First 50 Years

"A clear and concise book that will help any executive deliver a speech with confidence and clarity."
— Ken Bajaj, president,
Commerce One Global Services

"The tips in Joan Detz's book can help professionals deliver messages that work."
— Debbie Rosenberg Bush, director,
publications, Memorial Sloan-Kettering
Cancer Center

"It's not what you say, but who can help you say it better. And no one has better advice and more creative ideas than Joan Detz."
— A. W. "Bill" Dahlberg, chairman and CEO,
Southern Company

It's Not What You Say, It's How You Say It

ALSO BY JOAN DETZ

How to Write & Give a Speech

Can You Say a Few Words?

You Mean I Have to Stand Up and Say Something?

It's Not What You Say, It's How You Say It

Ready-to-Use Advice for Presentations, Speeches and
Other Speaking Occasions, Large and Small

Joan Detz

BRISTOL PARK BOOKS
NEW YORK

First Bristol Park Books edition published in 2007.

Published by Bristol Park Books
252 W. 38th Street
NYC, NY 10018

Bristol Park Books is a registered trademark of
Bristol Park Books, Inc.

Published by arrangement with St. Martin's Press.

ISBN 10: 0-88486-405-7
ISBN 13: 978-0-88486-405-9

Printed in the United States of America.

This is for my son, Seth . . .
who brings words to life every day,
and gives me great joy.

CONTENTS

SECTION ONE
What You Say
1

SECTION TWO
How You Say It
5

SECTION THREE
When You Say It
105

SECTION FOUR
Where You Say It
125

SECTION FIVE
Who Says It, and Who Is Listening?
139

SECTION SIX
Who Else Could Say It for You?
157

SECTION SEVEN
Was Your Speech a Success?
167

SECTION EIGHT
Appendix—Useful Books, Websites, and Professional Organizations
191

ACKNOWLEDGMENTS

I WOULD LIKE to thank my editor, Marian Lizzi. Marian knows books. Just as important, she knows authors. Her editorial decisions proved right on target—and her thoughtfulness made my work a pleasure.

To the booksellers who have carried my books over the years: a sincere "thank-you." I put myself through college by working in a bookstore—and I saw firsthand how you make a huge difference in the success of any book.

Along the same lines, I want to thank the librarians who have answered so many questions and been so supportive. I first learned to read by browsing the stacks at the Lancaster County (PA) Library—a Saturday ritual that shaped my childhood and ultimately formed a career. Every writer, and every reader, owes you a debt.

Special words for my family and friends: I know it was frustrating when you wanted to talk on the phone or meet for lunch—and I was forever "working on the book." Thank you for understanding how much I wanted to do this. Particular gratitude goes to Dominic Chianese, Patti Lauer, George and Nancy Miller, Walter Kaprielian, Joanna Bailes, Mary Jane Detz, and Rev. Nancy Sautter— for good cheer when it was most welcome.

But final tribute must go to my old cat, King Boy—who faithfully sat by my side as I wrote every book I've done over seventeen years. (While he never actually read any of my books, he seemed to take enormous delight in sitting on the paperwork.) This book was his last. King Boy died shortly after I finished this manuscript. There will be other cats and other books . . . but no more King Boy at my computer. So long, old boy. And thank you.

PREFACE

THIS BOOK OFFERS practical advice for anyone who ever has to say anything to anybody—which is to say, this book is for all of us.

The bottom line is: We all need to communicate. And we need to do it well if we're going to be successful—successful at work, at home, and in the community.

I hope this book will show you how to "say it better." Above all, I hope this book will help you feel more confident when you talk with other people.

The following pages are filled with real-life examples, practical tips, and podium-tested advice. You won't find any abstract theory here. Why? Because I'm not much of a "theory" person. And you know what? You're probably not a "theory" person, either.

If you're like most people, you want ready-to-use tips— practical speaking advice that you can put to good use right away. You'll get those communication skills from this book. And you'll gain the confidence that comes from knowing you can get your message across.

After all: *It's not what you say . . . it's how you say it.*
So read on.

"So shall my word be that goeth forth out of my mouth.
It shall not return to me void, but it shall accomplish that which
I please, and it shall prosper in the thing whereto I sent it."

—Isaiah 55:11, King James Version

"The real art of conversation is not only to say the
right thing in the right place, but, far more
difficult still, to leave unsaid the wrong thing at
the tempting moment."

—Lady Dorothy Nevill,
nineteenth-century English writer and socialite

"Speech is civilization itself."

—Thomas Mann

What You Say

"Blessed is the man who, having nothing to say, abstains from giving us wordy evidence of the fact."

—George Eliot, English novelist

■   ■   ■

■   ■   ■

THE TITLE OF THIS BOOK reads *It's Not What You Say, It's How You Say It*. But I have a confession: That might be a slight exaggeration. Because "what you say" *does* matter . . . it just doesn't tell the whole story.

Let me explain.

Maybe you have to run a community fund-raiser, or meet face-to-face with a sales prospect, or handle a tough job interview. Maybe you have to give a short presentation to a few colleagues at a department meeting, or give a big speech at a professional conference.

Whether you're talking to one person or a thousand, you certainly need a message. And that message must be targeted to your listeners' needs.

Before you decide "what to say," ask yourself these important questions:

(1) What do they *want* to hear from me?
(2) What do they *need* to hear from me?
    (Pamela Harriman, former U.S. ambassador to France, once defined leadership as "the ability to

tell people not what they want to hear, but what they need to know.")

(3) What do they already know about this topic—and where did they get their information?

(4) What misconceptions do they have?

(5) What problems do they face—and how did those problems develop?

(6) What solutions have they already tried?

(7) What message would be most comfortable?

(8) What message would be most troubling?

(9) What information could save them money?

(10) What information could save them time?

(11) What changes would I suggest they make?

(12) What recommendations could they put into practice most easily?

(13) What advice would be welcome?

(14) What advice would be resented?

(15) What perspective can I bring to their unique situation?

(16) And, perhaps the most important question: What can I say to them that no one else could say as effectively?

Once you ask yourself these basic questions, you should have a pretty good idea of what to say. And that's important, because you certainly need a message.

But good presentations demand more than a message. And that's why this chapter—the "content" chapter—is the shortest in the whole book. As you will soon see, good communication isn't just "what you say," it's *how* you say it.

How You Say It

"Whatever you do, kid, always serve it with a little dressing."

—George M. Cohan, theatrical producer

■   ■   ■

■　　■　　■

Choose Your Best Communication Option

This may sound like heresy coming from a speechwriter and speech coach, but giving a big speech isn't always the best way to sell your message. So before you automatically begin to prepare a formal presentation, ask yourself if an alternative method would work better.

George Washington didn't give his Farewell Address orally. Instead, Washington wrote the Address (with a little help from James Madison and Alexander Hamilton), and had it printed in a Philadelphia newspaper.

Consider your own alternatives, as well.

- **face-to-face**

One-on-one communication is both personal and persuasive. Longtime Kentucky senator Wendell H. Ford didn't waste much time giving speeches on the floor of the Senate. As he put it: "Why make a speech when you can sit down with your colleagues and work something out?"

• talking points

Maybe you shouldn't prepare a fully written text for the speech. Informal notes might be more flexible and serve you better. This improvisational style has worked well for Secretary of State Madeleine K. Albright. She may start with basic talking points, but as the dialogue progresses, she then expounds the U.S. position.

• question-and-answer sessions

A Q&A format gets your message out and also lets you respond to the unique needs of each audience. One caution: Handling a Q&A session takes great skill, and you'll need to practice.

• public appearances

Sometimes, just being seen is enough—and it's certainly a lot less work. President Bill Clinton seemed nonplussed when the public-address system failed during his scheduled speech at the Little Rock, Arkansas, airport. Ditching the broken microphone, Clinton just laughed and hollered to the audience, "So what? I didn't want to give a speech today anyway!" With that, Clinton pleased the crowd by signing autographs.

• silence

When Frank Sinatra died, Las Vegas honored the singer by dimming its lights. For one minute, the Las Vegas Strip slowed its pace and paid its respects to the legend who had drawn millions to his shows.

• voice-mail messages

Do you want to nip rumors in the bud? Consider using an all-employee voice-mail message—an effective and fast technique to inform a lot of people at the same time.

• e-mail messages

Rather than holding a traditional press conference, Judge Hiller B. Zobel effectively used e-mail to announce his decision in the highly publicized trial of British au pair Louise Woodward. His unprecedented use of e-mail in 1997 made the text of his ruling instantly available on the World Wide Web.

- **reports**

Complex material might work better in a written report—where readers can take all the time they need to comprehend the details.

- **letters**

Want to share confidential information? Persuade? Apologize? A personal letter might work better than a public presentation—allowing readers to digest the message in a private atmosphere.

- **op-ed pieces**

Need to address an important community issue? Rather than just giving a speech to forty people at a local meeting, you can reach thousands by writing an op-ed piece for the newspaper.

Think of your options as a "communication toolbox." Here's what I mean:

Did you ever notice that plumbers bring huge toolkits to every job? They typically wind up using only one or two tools, but they bring the entire kit because they never know what will work best in a given situation.

Well, that's exactly how *you* need to think about communication skills. No "magic method" will work in every situation, but if you have a variety of communication tools in your "skills box," you'll be prepared for any event.

So, review your options, and then decide the best way to communicate your message. But once you commit to giving a presentation, you must remember: it's not just what you say, it's how you say it.

Here are some important factors that will determine how you develop your speech.

How Long Should You Talk?

*"There's great power in words,
if you don't hitch too many of them together."*
—JOSH BILLINGS, NINETEENTH CENTURY HUMORIST

Business executives often ask me, "How long should I make my presentation?" My answer is simple: "How short can you make it?" In other words, if you can get your message across in fifteen minutes, why take thirty-five? To sound more intelligent? To "impress" your audience? To show how hard you worked?

Think again.

Think like Muriel Humphrey, wife of Senator Hubert Humphrey. Reflecting on her husband's penchant for talking on and on, Muriel once commented, "Hubert, a speech does not have to be eternal to be immortal."

The truth is, no one likes a speech that runs too long. Even if your speech is interesting, the audience will want it to end. (Of course, if your speech is boring, the audience will want it to end even sooner.)

In 1841, President William Harrison gave the longest presidential inaugural address ever—running on for nearly two hours (during a snowstorm, no less)—wearing no hat and no coat. President Harrison died of pneumonia a month later. There's got to be a lesson in that somewhere.

"I'm convinced someday there will be a president who announces his program in less than twenty minutes. I don't care if he's Democrat or Republican, I'm going to support him."
—SENATOR ORRIN HATCH, COMMENTING ON PRESIDENT CLINTON'S SEVENTY-SEVEN-MINUTE STATE OF THE UNION ADDRESS IN 1999

Unfortunately, length is the most misunderstood aspect of giving a presentation. Speakers are typically given a time frame ("Can you speak for an hour at the next Chamber of Commerce meeting?")—and they tend to fill whatever time frame they're given.

That's reactive, not *pro*active. And that's just not smart.

If you want to get an audience on your side, you need to choose the right length of time for your message. How can you make that decision? Well, there is no generic answer. You must analyze each situation.

One popular preacher turned to Divine guidance, offering this silent prayer every time he approached the pulpit: "Lord, fill my mouth with worthwhile stuff . . . and nudge me when I've said enough."

But if you want something a bit more concrete, take this practical approach: Suppose you are invited to speak at a conference. A program coordinator will typically suggest a specific length for your presentation—let's say, forty-five minutes. Nod your head, appear appreciative, say thank you . . . and then totally disregard whatever time frame they gave you.

Why? Because program coordinators are trained to think in "time slots." That is, they might need a speaker to fill their agenda from 1:30 to 2:15 P.M. Fine. Maybe you will be that speaker. But good speeches do more than fill time slots. As the invited speaker, your job is to communicate a message—and to captivate the audience while you do it.

So don't automatically prepare a forty-five minute speech just because they give you a forty-five minute time frame. Use this checklist to determine the best length.

_____ **Consider the setting.** Is it inside or outside? air-conditioned or not? spacious or crowded? standing room or comfortable seats? Never forget: It's hard to communicate with an audience when they are uncomfortable. If you talk too long, they will tune you out.

_____ **Ask to see an agenda for the entire conference.**

_____ **Study the amount of time given to other speakers.** Are you being asked to speak longer or shorter? Why? [NOTE: Section Three will give you lots of practical tips for choosing the best spot on an agenda.]

_____ **Find out what precedes your speech.** For example, if you're scheduled to talk right after lunch, understand that lunch often runs overtime and so you might get less time to deliver your talk.

_____ **Find out what follows your speech.** Be realistic. If your speech is followed by a cocktail hour, the audience will be itching to get out of there.

_____ **Always factor in a few minutes for starting late.** It's a rare conference that stays on schedule. Technical glitches eat up time. Coffee breaks have a mysterious way of expanding. Other speakers run late. Don't assume you will get all the time you've been promised. (I was once asked to prepare a two-hour workshop for a professional conference—only to learn upon arrival that the conference was running way behind schedule, and would I please cut my remarks to thirty minutes!)

_____ **Ask if you must share your time slot with anyone.** [NOTE: You can learn more about panels in Section Six.]

_____ **Consider the complexity of your material.** Rather than taking an extra ten minutes to explain complex information, offer handouts that illustrate your points with charts and graphs. The audience will appreciate the chance to study this material afterward.

_____ **Consider the emotional fabric of the event.** Will the listeners be sad? Angry? Frustrated? Don't foist a lengthy lecture on them.

_____ **Factor in time for personal comments.** When James Coburn won his first Academy Award at age seventy, he naturally had a lot of things to say. Although his acceptance speech ran short of time, he still managed to thank his wife, who "finally got to come to the Academy Awards."

_____ **Allow time for someone to introduce you.**

_____ **Allow time for distributing any handouts.**

_____ **Allow time for a question-and-answer session.**

_____ **Allow time for exchanging business cards after the presentation.**

_____ **Allow time for selling any books or materials.**

Now can you see how preparing a forty-five-minute speech just because you've been given a forty-five-minute time slot would be a big mistake? A twenty-minute speech might serve everyone better—allowing ample time for a good introduction, a lively Q&A, and some terrific networking.

Use this as a basic rule of thumb: **The more you say, the less people remember.** (Or, as Dan Quayle put it so well, "Verbosity leads to unclear, inarticulate things.")

How to Organize Your Message

> *"The mind has its own logic but does not often let others in on it."*
> —BERNARD AUGUSTINE DE VOTO

Too many speakers have their own "logic"—but unfortunately, they don't let others in on it. Is it any wonder that listeners often sit there in utter confusion? Every message needs a beginning, a middle, and an ending. And it's your job, as presenter, to convey that structure to the listeners.

Don't worry about finding the "best" way to organize your material. That's a waste of time because there is no best way. Instead, you'll find lots of *good* ways. Just pick whatever suits your speaking style and your material—and be sure to make your organization clear, so the audience can follow along.

Listeners need to know, right from the beginning, how you plan to proceed. Here are some formats that work well.

- **chronological order**
Frame your material in a time line—year by year, quar-

ter by quarter, month by month, et cetera. Create a powerful sense of immediacy by giving your audience a day-by-day look at the activities of your school, or an hour-by-hour glimpse into the workings of your company.

- **pros and cons**

Outline the advantages and the disadvantages. Be candid: Don't gloss over the disadvantages. Audiences always spot these weaknesses anyway, so you might as well be the first to point them out. Your honesty will build credibility.

- **problems and solutions**

Got a problem? Describe it in clear, factual terms. Point out the ramifications. Put a dollar figure on the costs. Cite the toll on human resources. Above all, let the audience "see" how this problem affects their lives. Then offer some solutions.

Don't be vague. Spell things out. Say, "I'm going to present three possible solutions, and then we can break into small groups to discuss the merits of each solution."

- **compare and contrast**

Which idea/program/product is better? How are they similar? Where do they differ? Which costs more money? Which saves more time? Provide objective facts, but also share your own opinions. As Mark Twain put it, "It is the difference of opinion that makes horse races."

- **alphabetical order**

Putting lists in alphabetical order is particularly helpful when you're using slides. The audience can see at a glance exactly what you've covered and how many additional points you plan to address.

- **numerical order**

Make your format clear by saying, "Today I'm going to talk about our five goals for the coming year." Then address each goal in order. By using a numerical listing (goal number 1, goal number 2, and so on), you make it very easy for an audience to follow along.

TIP: Make your first point the shortest. Why? Because you want to create a sense of progress early in the speech. If you linger too long on the first point, your audience will get restless. They will mentally calculate the length of your speech: "Hmm. We've already spent six minutes on the first point, and we've got nine more points to go. It's going to take forever to get out of here." This is hardly the way to build audience rapport.

(CAUTION: Be extra careful in numbering your points. If you accidentally omit number 3, or repeat number 5 twice, you will lose credibility.)

- **order of importance**

By putting your most important point first, you accomplish a few things.

(1) You make sure you get that point across. After all, you might plan a twenty-minute presentation but wind up with only seven minutes because another panelist ran overtime. If you can't communicate your entire message, at least you can make your most important point.

(2) By stressing the most important point first, you send a clear (if unstated) message to the audience: "This matters. Pay attention."

(3) You eliminate ambiguity. The audience knows where you stand right away.

- **psychological order**

Do you anticipate resistance? Skepticism? Mistrust? If so, make a psychological appeal to your audience. Put your most acceptable material at the beginning so everyone can agree on something right up front. Once your audience agrees on one point, they will be more likely to support your other points.

• **geographic order**

Take your audience from north to south, east to west, state to state, or country to country. By moving geographically, you add structure to your message, making it easier for listeners to follow and to comprehend. As an added plus, the geographical movement builds visual appeal, which can be helpful with audio-visual aids.

• **question-and-answer format**

No time to prepare a formal presentation? Here's an easy tip: Pick the five or ten most common questions about your topic, and use them to structure your message. For example—"As I travel around the country, employees ask many questions about the competition we face. Today, I'd like to give you the top ten questions I hear . . . and share my responses with you." With this easy-to-use structure in place, your presentation will almost prepare itself.

No matter what format you use, make sure it's clear to the audience. Remember: Speakers never get a second chance. The audience either "gets it" the first time, or they don't get it at all. That means you have to organize things very clearly. Use the following checklist to evaluate your organization.

ORGANIZATION

Identify your organizational strengths:

_____ I open with an effective grabber.

_____ I have a clear purpose.

_____ I use an easy-to-follow structure.

_____ I emphasize my main points.

_____ I provide an appropriate amount of supporting material.

_____ I stay within the time frame.

_____ I summarize my key points.

_____ I give a memorable conclusion.

IDEAS FOR MORE CREATIVE ORGANIZATION

Be as creative with your structure as you like. Here are some examples to inspire you.

* When Dave Thomas, the founder of Wendy's International, spoke about success at Hillsdale College, he organized his "ingredients for success" into four basic groups—echoing the four basic food groups. These "ingredients" formed the structure of his entire speech.
* When comedian Bob Newhart delivered the one-hundredth commencement address at Catholic University of America, he used a very loose structure—essentially stringing together a series of humorous anecdotes to illustrate his theme, *Humor Makes Us Free.*

HOW TO OPEN

You've got about thirty seconds to grab the audience's attention. Use those thirty seconds well. Pick something specific that will pique their interest. Try using

* a startling statistic
* a real-life example

* a human-interest story
* a humorous anecdote
* a clever definition
* a funny quotation
* a rhetorical question
* a reference to current events
* a reference to the organization
* even a reference to the weather

A few words of caution:

- **Do not open with vague statements.** Audiences dislike ho-hum generalities, and they will turn you off.
- **Do not take too long to make your first point.** The audience will get restless, you will lose momentum, and your delivery will suffer.
- **Do not open with a joke.** Unless you are a professional comedian, this is too much of a gamble. There's nothing worse than a joke that falls flat—unless it's a joke that falls flat at the beginning of a presentation. When that happens, you have to dig yourself out of a hole—hardly an effective way to project confidence and credibility.

How to Close

Here's the good news: Closing a speech isn't so hard. Even if a speech is interesting, most audiences welcome the wrap-up. Why? So they can go to the bathroom, or get a cup of coffee, or return to work. Of course, if your speech is boring, the audience is absolutely dying to hear your ending! Either way, it's hard to go wrong when you close.

But there's bad news, too: Once you begin to wrap up your presentation, you need to move swiftly. If you take too long to summarize your points, you will annoy the audience. Most dangerous? Actually saying, "In conclusion . . ." Once you utter these powerful words, you've got about thirty seconds to clear the platform-tops. I once witnessed a speaker who said "in conclusion" three times. It wasn't a pretty sight.

How to Do Terrific Research

"In this life we want nothing but Facts, sir,
nothing but Facts."
—CHARLES DICKENS

Research. The word alone turns off many people. In fact, doing research often ranks as the most dreaded part of a speaking assignment. Most people like it about as much as they like root canals. That's unfortunate, because research doesn't have to be boring; quite the opposite, research can be creative, intellectually stimulating, and downright fun.

Doing the research doesn't have to be time-consuming, either. There's no law that says you have to spend hours on the Internet, or getting lost in the maze of the Dewey decimal system. Research can be as simple as talking with employees in your company cafeteria or scanning some letters from community leaders.

So why do most speakers dislike research? For starters, they limit themselves. They automatically equate "research" with "statistics," and they assume statistics have to be boring.

Well, those people haven't heard the right statistics. Let me give you some guidelines and some good examples.

HOW TO TAKE DULL STATISTICS AND MAKE THEM INTERESTING

- **Simplify your numbers.** Don't say, "Our state is growing so fast that we need to add 2.91 new classrooms every day." Round up the number to say "three classrooms." (Rounded numbers are easier for you to deliver—and infinitely easier for your audience to comprehend.)

- **Put your numbers in perspective.** When Barbara Bush spoke about illiteracy, she urged audiences to "turn off the TV. The average kindergarten student has watched more than five thousand hours of television. That's more time than it takes to earn a college degree."

- **Create a picture with numbers.** Some ideas:
  * "The unnecessary paperwork would fill X number of boxes."
  * "The wasted food would fill X number of refrigerators."
  * "The money lost because of excessive absentism would be enough to hire X number of employees."

- **Put your numbers in human terms.** Show how your numbers impact real people. For example: "This highway would shorten your commute by fifteen minutes." The more you relate numbers to everyday lives, the more folks will listen to you.

- **Create a sense of immediacy.** Put statistics in the context of "this day" or "this hour" or "this minute." For example: "We've all gathered at this conference to talk about teenage drinking. During the hour it takes to hold this panel, X number of teens in our state will drink alcohol. Some of them will get behind the wheel of a car. Will you meet one of them on the road when you're driving home today?"

- **Limit your use of statistics.** There's no sense inundating your audience with a plethora of numbers; if you give them too many, they won't remember any. A smarter choice? Use only a few statistics, but make those numbers especially interesting.

RESEARCH OPTIONS

Yes, statistics are important. And when you handle them well, they can be incredibly interesting. But, again, statistics are not your only research option. In fact, the more experienced you become at giving presentations, the less you will rely on statistics—and the more you will use other options.

Variety is the key to good research. Try using a combination of the following:

- **anecdotes**

You have two choices: You can either search for a good anecdote in a reference collection, or you can tell an anecdote based on personal experience (perhaps something you saw on the way to work or heard at the gym). Either way, you'll have a memorable bit of research to share with your audience.

- **anniversaries**

The tenth year of your organization? The one-hundredth year of your company? Make good use of these anniversaries to put your message in perspective.

- **biblical references**

Look for short, memorable lines. (The Book of Proverbs is a particularly great source—and many of them make great titles, too.) But, use caution: Citing individual Bible verses out of context can backfire, as then president Ronald Reagan learned when he cited Luke 14:31 to support his proposal for increasing the military budget. Although Reagan said, "The Scriptures are on our side," church scholars thought differently—and did not hesitate to say so.

- **cartoons**

A talented artist can create cartoons to illustrate your key points. (CAUTION: Published cartoons are protected by copyright and may not be copied without permission.)

- **case histories**

Because case histories have a beginning, a middle, and an ending, they are easy for speakers to deliver. You won't need to rely on your notes so much. Even more important, case histories are easy for listeners to remember. After leaving, your audience can readily retell the information to their colleagues.

- **charts, graphs, and tables**

Complex material? Let a good chart convey your information.

- **comparison and contrast**

Someone once asked singer Kenny Rogers why he chose to invest in Branson, Missouri. His response? "The Grand Canyon has four million visitors a year. . . . Five million people will come to Branson this year."

- **community issues**

Can you tie in your message to local situations? local problems? local programs? Do so—you'll make a stronger impact.

- **corporate history**

How has your company grown? What makes your employees feel proud? Where have you made the biggest impact? By sharing your corporate history with the audience, you will also share your corporate pride.

- **customer comments**

Cite recent letters or phone calls from customers. Share surveys. Interview employees who answer the phones. Let the audience know what's on your customers' minds.

- **date in history**

Giving a speech on June 23? Find out what happened on that date in history, and look for a connection with your topic. [NOTE: In the appendix in Section Eight, I mention some reference sources that provide these calendar listings.] When Elie Wiesel received the Congressional Medal of Achievement, he reminded the audience of what had happened on that particular date in history: On April 19, 1943, the Warsaw ghetto rose up to fight the Nazis.

- **definitions**

People love witty definitions. Turn to the reference books listed in the appendix in Section Eight to find definitions such as these:

- * *problem*—"an opportunity in work clothes" (Henry Kaiser II)
- * *science*—"piecemeal revelation" (Oliver Wendell Holmes)
- * *insurance*—"an ingenuous modern game of chance in which the player is permitted to enjoy the comfortable conviction that he is beating the man who keeps the table" (Ambrose Bierce)
- * *success*—"not to get ahead of other people, but to get ahead of ourselves" (Malthie Babcock)

Or, make up your own definitions, as Ann Richards, the former State Treasurer of Texas, did in her feisty keynote address to the Democratic National Convention. She began by defining the Reagan-Bush era this way: "I want to announce to this nation that in a little more than one hundred days, the Reagan–Meese–Deaver–Nofzier–Poindexter –North–Weinberger–Watt–Gorsuch–Lavell–Stockman– Haig–Bork–Noriega–George Bush era will be over."

- **demonstrations**

Show-and-tell worked wonders in elementary school. It still does. Audiences may forget what you *tell* them, but they will not easily forget what you *show* them.

- **descriptions**

Create a *mental* picture for your audience. Use vivid descriptions to let them "see" your topic.

- **details**

Don't talk in generalizations—heed Sherlock Holmes: "Never trust impressions, my boy, but concentrate yourself upon details."

- **employee comments**

Good sources include the employee suggestion box, postings on bulletin boards, Intranet comments, letters to the employee newspaper.

- **endorsements**

Who likes your project? Why? When did they learn about it? How did it help them? What were the benefits? A first-person endorsement packs great credibility.

- **ethnic folktales**

When Governor Mario Cuomo spoke at Syracuse University following the crash of Pan Am 101, he touched the emotions of the audience by including a Yiddish folktale. [Again, the appendix in Section Eight lists good sources of regional and ethnic material.]

- **examples**

One good example is worth more than a hundred generalizations. Albert Einstein called examples "the only way of educating." Who's to argue?

• **experts**

Make sure you choose experts who will be credible to your audience. Keep in mind that each audience has different standards of credibility. Sorry, you won't find a "one size fits all" expert. The reality is, an authority who impresses one audience may fail with another. (The poet Carl Sandburg put it colorfully when he described an "expert" as "a damned fool a long way from home.")

• **facts**

In isolation, facts lack meaning, so always pay attention to context. Aldous Huxley said facts are "ventriloquist's dummies. Sitting on a wise man's knee they may be made to utter words of wisdom; elsewhere, they say nothing." Make sure your facts are sitting on a "wise man's knee."

• **family history**

Family details humanize the speaker and reach the audience on an emotional level. When David Dinkins became the first black mayor of New York City in 1990, he told the audience that his ancestors were brought to America in the hold of a slave ship: "We have not finished the journey toward liberty and justice, but surely we have come a long way."

• **geographical information**

Doing business in Singapore? Brussels? Mexico City? Include some details that offer local color.

• **illustrations**

Consider artwork or photographs to illustrate your main points.

• **letters from constituents (customers, shareholders, students, parents, voters, et cetera)**

This was a favorite technique of President Reagan, who would reach into his pocket in the middle of a speech, unfold a letter with perfect timing, and then share it with the rest of the world.

- **news stories**

Just sit down with a notepad and watch the evening news on TV. Chances are, you'll find something to mention in your presentation.

- **personal observations**

Ben Jonson once said, "I do love to note and to observe." Audiences may not always agree with your personal observations, but when you share your perspective, you share a piece of your personality—and this does a great deal to build audience rapport.

- **polls**

Consider the possible range—everything from national political polls to local polls on community issues. Can't find a poll that reflects your issue? Do your own.

- **pop culture**

Make a reference to a hit movie. Play with the title of a best-selling book. Paraphrase a popular song.

- **proverbs**

Proverbs say much with few words—and say it quite well. Francis Bacon described proverbs as "pointed speeches." You will want to have several reference sources for finding these little gems.

- **quotations**

Audiences love quotations—and so do speakers. But a few guidelines are in order.

> * Avoid the obvious. If you're talking about the environment, for example, don't just quote the Environmental Protection Agency. Consider using comments

from an activist, a corporate scientist, an academic, a farmer, the Bible, a national news magazine, or a waste management company.

* Avoid repetition. Don't quote Benjamin Franklin (or anyone else) a half dozen times in a speech.

* Avoid a complicated quotation. Keep it short and sharp. Cut (or paraphrase) any slow parts.

* Blend the quotation into your speech. Please don't say, "quote . . . unquote." Instead, pause a moment, change your tone, then let your voice show you're giving a quote.

* You must be comfortable with the quotation. If you trip over words, the message will be lost.

* Pronounce the source's name correctly. I once heard a speaker pronounce "Voltaire" as "Vol-ta-ree." It's awfully hard to project credibility when you can't say a name properly.

* Use quotes *sparingly*—the audience wants to hear *your* thoughts.

• **research studies**

Up-to-the-minute research can be very impressive. But remember: Summarize the research in easy-to-understand terms. Your presentation should not sound like an academic treatise.

• **statistics**

In a speech at American University, Massachusetts senator Ted Kennedy stressed the importance of spending money to improve children's education and health. Kennedy urged $5 billion in federal funds—emphasizing that this figure was a mere "six days' cost of running the Department of Defense."

- **testimonials**

Study good TV commercials, and learn from their time-honored techniques. Give your audience a "slice of life" glimpse into your topic. Use real faces, real voices, real problems, real solutions.

- **video clips**

Fund-raising for a community project? Urging employees to support the United Way? Getting students to help with a senior-citizen project? Don't rely solely on your own words. Show them short video clips. Let them see the people who need their help.

WHAT NOT TO INCLUDE

A civic leader once solicited public support for a controversial proposal by using this rationale: "It's what we've been doing for thirty years." Not surprisingly, his rationale failed to pass muster.

If you can't find a better reason than "it's the way we've always done it," you have two options: (1) do more research to find a better reason; or (2) give up. Just because you've done something the same way for thirty years doesn't mean it's the best way to do things in the future.

How to Use Storytelling Techniques

"Nobody ever sold anybody anything
by boring them to death."
—DAVID OGILVY

How can storytelling techniques improve a business presentation? For starters, audiences love to hear a good story, so give them something they will enjoy. Also, audiences pay attention to stories. They may tune out dry statistics, but their ears perk up with the very prospect of a story. Audiences remember stories. After they leave your presentation, they may not remember all your facts, but they will enthusiastically retell your tales to their colleagues. On a deeper level, stories help get the audience on your side. They let you share a bit of your own personality. What better way to build a rapport with your audience?

But storytelling is much more than entertainment. The truth is, stories are a sound educational technique. We learn through stories. And master teachers have always known this. Jesus taught by telling parables. Jewish families cherish the Passover tradition of reading the story about the Exodus from Egypt. All major religions share their richness and nourish their traditions through storytelling.

Smart ministers lace their sermons with stories. Smart professors keep huge lecture halls awake with stories. Smart trial lawyers sway juries with stories. And smart business executives can do the same.

Because stories are concrete, they communicate your message better than generalizations. Also, because stories are personalized, they build credibility better than abstract statements.

To summarize the benefits: Audiences like information that's presented in story form. They grasp it quicker. They trust it more. They repeat it more accurately. They share it more readily. They relay it more enthusiastically. And they remember it longer.

Do you really need any more reasons to include story-telling in your next presentation?

How to Improve Your Speechwriting Skills

I've been writing speeches professionally for twenty years. Along the way, I've refined some techniques that help me polish my own writing. Here are some practical suggestions that may work for you as well.

- **Read it aloud.** You can't really tell how something will sound until . . . well, until you hear it. So don't wait until you're at the podium. Read your speech manuscript aloud as you work on it. You'll prevent a lot of unpleasant surprises. (You'll also do a better job of timing your presentation.)
- **Print hard copy along the way.** Don't edit or proofread on the computer screen. Studies show that computer rewrites take much longer; even worse, they are less successful. So print your manuscript as you go—and do your editing on paper.
- **Look for short paragraphs.** Speakers tend to pause at paragraph breaks, so using more frequent indentations helps ensure more frequent pauses. Also, long paragraphs are harder to deliver because speakers "get lost" in the morass of words.
- **Look for periods.** The more, the better. Why? Because frequent periods indicate short sentences. Short sentences are easier for a speaker to deliver, and easier for an audience to understand.

- **Beware commas.** By definition, commas connect grammatical units. If you spot lots of commas on a page, it's a sign you're using lots of complex grammatical constructions. Give your audience a break. Cut. Simplify.

- **Try to find some question marks.** If you don't find any, that means you're not using any rhetorical questions. Do a quick rewrite—strategically adding rhetorical questions throughout your presentation to involve the audience. (BONUS: By asking rhetorical questions, you instinctively improve your eye contact.)

- **Look for quotation marks.** They indicate dialogue—a surefire way to make your presentation sound more conversational.

- **Value verbs.** They inject energy and add spunk. When I teach speechwriting seminars, I include a critique exercise where I ask participants to identify the verbs in their speech manuscript. Are they using active verbs? Great. Active verbs convey *action*—and presentations thrive on movement. Unfortunately, too many speechwriters rely on passive verbs—the weakest form of verbs in the entire language. Don't get me wrong. I'm not saying passive verbs are bad; I'm just saying they're weak. If you use too many passive verbs, you'll have a weak presentation.

  WEAK: "Our sales goals were achieved."
  STRONGER: "We hit our goals."

- **Avoid overusing "is," "are," "was," "were."** Cross out forms of the verb "to be," and see if you can replace them with more dynamic verbs.

  WEAK: "Offering quality daycare is a way to improve employee morale."

STRONGER: "Offering quality daycare boosts employee morale."

- **Cut hidden verbs.** Replace them with bold, precise verbs. Remember: The stronger the verb, the stronger the speaker.

  WEAK: "We have now come to the realization that . . ."

  STRONGER: "We now realize . . ."

- **Use vivid words.** Former New York governor Mario Cuomo has earned a reputation as one of the best speakers in the country. Listen carefully to his speeches and you'll find the secret: vivid words—colorful, feisty, sometimes irreverent, always lively. Consider how Cuomo conveyed these statistics to the 1992 National Democratic Convention:

  "Today, a $400 billion annual deficit and a $4 trillion national debt hang like great albatrosses around the nation's neck—strangling our economy, menacing our future."

- **Count syllables.** Do most of your words have three, four, or five syllables? If so, you're in trouble. It's often hard for a speaker to pronounce multisyllabic words. And it's very hard for an audience to comprehend them. So hit that DELETE button and find shorter words.

- **Avoid sexist or biased language.** Try these simple techniques.

  * *Use a different word.*

anchorman	=	anchor, newscaster
businessman	=	business executive
chairman	=	chair
fireman	=	firefighter

gentleman's agreement	=	unwritten agreement
handicapped	=	people with disabilities
man-made	=	synthetic
spokesman	=	spokesperson; represen-tative
waitress	=	server

* *Rewrite in the plural.*

BIASED: "Give each employee his notebook when he returns from his lunch."

BETTER: "Give the employees their notebooks when they return from lunch."

CLUMSY: "Each applicant must submit his or her form by June 3."

BETTER: "Applicants must submit their forms by June 3."

* *Be specific.*

VAGUE: "Senior citizens will get a 10 percent discount."

BETTER: "Anyone over fifty-five will get a 10 percent discount."

* *Use the second person ("you").*

BIASED: "An applicant can contact his manager."

DIRECT: "You can contact your manager."

- **Think positive.** Rewrite the negative. EASY TIP: Search for *no*, *not*, and *none*. When you find these negative words, reread the whole sentence—then try to find a better way to say it.

BEFORE: "The advisory board was not united."

AFTER: "The advisory board was divided."

- **Beware the "weakeners."** Certain introductory phases ("there are," "there is") weaken sentences. Rewrite to omit.

BEFORE: "There are only a handful of banks that are currently able to leverage their information."

AFTER: "Only a handful of banks leverage their information."

- **Watch the use of "that."** Cut it whenever possible.

  BEFORE: "This is the issue that I want to address today."

  AFTER: "This is the issue I want to address."

- **Avoid qualifiers:** "I think . . ." "We believe . . ." They sound wishy-washy. Cut them; your sentences will be shorter and stronger, and you will sound more confident.

  BEFORE: "We believe that our winning strategy is to focus on the needs of our customers."

  AFTER: "Our winning strategy focuses on our customers."

- **Avoid jargon.** Go on a "search-and-destroy mission" for bureaucratic gobbledygook and stuffy legalese. Replace with plain English.

LEGALESE	PLAIN ENGLISH
"in view of the fact that"	"because"
"in accordance with the issued request"	"as you requested"
"the aforementioned proposal, which we are in receipt of"	"the proposal we received"
"maximize"	"build"
"conceptualize"	"imagine," "think about"
"utilize"	"use"

- **Cut redundancy.**

"totally complete"	=	"complete"
"future plans"	=	"plans"
"carefully examine"	=	"examine"

- **Tighten your quotes.** You're giving a presentation, not a doctoral dissertation. You don't have to include every single word of every single quote. Edit, cut. Drop anything that interferes with the essential meaning of your quote. You goal? Making the quote easy for the audience to hear . . . and easy for the audience to remember.
- **Use parallel structure.** It just sounds better. And it improves audience comprehension.

President Lyndon Johnson: "Aggression unchallenged is aggression unleashed."
President John F. Kennedy: "If a free society cannot help the many who are poor, it cannot save the few who are rich."

How to Improve Your Delivery Skills

"Styles, like everything else, change. Style doesn't."
—LINDA ELLERBEE, TELEVISION JOURNALIST

Here are some of the most common delivery issues, arranged alphabetically so you can find your problem area quickly.

AD-LIBS

Sure, you can plan all you want. But the truth is, when you speak, you often face the unexpected. A clever ad-lib may be your salvation.

Dr. Bryant Kirkland was renowned for giving great sermons at Fifth Avenue Presbyterian Church in New York

City. I loved listening to him. One Sunday morning his sermon was interrupted by a honking car. I watched Dr. Kirkland ignore the car horn for a moment, but then he paused, smiled, and told the congregation, "Will somebody let that fellow in, whoever he is? [Pause.] And give him a Bible, too!" The congregation laughed . . . and the minister moved on, with our full attention.

Consider one speaker, who faced a nonfunctioning sound system at a school meeting. Instead of getting flustered, she used her loudest voice to ask if the audience could hear her. And with a smile, she hollered her response: "See? When you're a mom, you just learn to make yourself heard over the noise."

Make a list of possible glitches and arm yourself with some clever one-liners. As all experienced speakers know, the best ad-libs are the ones you've planned for.

* If dishes drop during a luncheon address, don't miss a beat. Gesture, and offer, "For those of you who think *that's* hard to do, just try standing up here!"
* If you suddenly hear raucous noise from an adjacent room, say, "Well, it sounds like the sales team is prepping for another banner year."
* If you continue to be bothered by noise from other quarters, take it in stride with, "Don't worry. In this industry, we're used to competition."
* If you trip over words, pause a moment to collect your thoughts, then say, "Let me offer an instant replay, for those of you who don't happen to speak garble."
* If something interferes with the agenda (a P.A. announcement, a late speaker, an unwanted delivery), show your confidence by saying, "I'm not worried.

Really. This is all part of the program. [Pause.] It's the part we didn't rehearse."

The award for Most Creative Ad-lib goes to former president George Bush, who was once confronted by an AIDS activist waving an unrolled condom. The president somehow managed this line: "Oh. New press credentials."

APPLAUSE

> *"Listen to them when they are reacting as a*
> *mass—never listen to an individual reaction."*
> —RICHARD RODGERS, GIVING ADVICE ON
> AUDIENCES

* When Pope John Paul II made his final appearance during a visit to Mexico, the emotional crowd gave him a fifteen minute ovation.
* When German chancellor Helmut Kohl faced a supportive crowd in Berlin, the audience repeatedly chanted his name.
* When Lyndon Johnson campaigned from a flatbed truck traveling across the small towns of Texas, the applause was often deafening.
* When Jesse Jackson spoke at the Democratic convention, the audience stood up—cheering with gusto.
* When Wayne Gretzky played his final hockey game in his native Canada, fans greeted him with a seventeen-minute ovation.

While you might not get such an enthusiastic response, you should certainly prepare yourself for some applause. At the very least, your audience will applaud at the end. Even if you're not very good, an audience will applaud just because they're glad when a speech is over.

The only exception I can think of is if you happen to be the president of the United States and there are members of the Supreme Court in your audience. According to tradition, Supreme Court justices remain silent. They do not applaud or cheer. And they most assuredly do not chant. But aside from this rarefied group, audiences applaud.

Indeed, if your presentation is good, the audience will applaud enthusiastically—even interrupting you at the parts they like the best. (TIP: Audiences typically applaud at your most pleasing material. Pay attention. Learn from their reaction. And include more of this popular material in your next speech.) In particular, pay close attention to *when* and *how long* your audience applauds.

Fulton J. Sheen shared these thoughts about applause: "At the start of a lecture, it is a manifestation of faith. If it comes in the middle, a sign of hope. At the end, it is always charity." No matter when you hear the applause, be sure to stop a moment, nod in appreciation, and then move on as the clapping subsides.

Of course, if you don't want to take any chances, you can always bring your applause with you. When President George Bush gave his first speech to the General Assembly at the United Nations, Barbara Bush sat in the gallery, leading the applause. You can follow suit. Bring some of your own supporters to an important speech, to initiate applause. Just make sure they're carefully seated throughout the room. If all of your colleagues are lined up in one row, clapping in unison . . . well, it looks a bit phony.

AUDIOVISUAL SUPPORT

> *"Let our advance worrying become advance*
> *thinking and planning."*
> —SIR WINSTON CHURCHILL

When the Ava Gardner Museum in Smithfield, North Carolina, planned a benefit screening, they opened the film canister and found it contained the wrong film. Fortunately, these folks had the good sense to check their AV materials *before* the audience arrived.

Unfortunately, not every speaker takes these precautions. And that's why frustrated audiences often find themselves staring at an upside-down slide, a blank screen, out-of-order transparencies, or fizzled Power Point presentations.

That's also why frustrated speakers often watch their AV fall to pieces because of something as simple as a burned-out lightbulb, or a missing electrical cord, or too-small typeface. Even the fanciest AV presentation will fail unless you follow a few basic guidelines.

* Keep the words on your slides to a minimum. Think of the screen like a highway billboard ad, or a bumper sticker, or a T-shirt slogan—easy to read and easy to remember.
* Avoid inundating your audience with too many numbers. I've seen slides that had dozens of numbers, and when I walked away, I couldn't remember a single one.
* Avoid overwhelming your audience with too many slides. One presenter tried to cram seventy-five slides into an hour. He moved the slides so quickly that they

almost seemed like a movie—a very bad movie, I might add.

* Unless you are planning to offer binoculars, use a typeface that's big enough to be seen from the back of the room.

* Presenting in English—or any other read-left-to-right language? Then stand stage right.

* Don't read what's on the screen. Slides should supplement what you say—not repeat it. The audience didn't come so you could read out loud to them. They came to hear you explain things in your own words.

* Don't turn your back to the audience when you gesture to the screen. They didn't come to stare at your shoulder blades. A better choice: Keep the screen on *your* left so you can easily point to the slide by extending your left hand.

* Unless you plan to amuse your audience with a shadow-puppet extravaganza, never block the light source when you gesture.

* Use a remote control to advance the slides. If you must rely on a second person, avoid constantly saying, "May I have the next slide, please?" This merely makes you sound like a broken record—a very annoying broken record.

* Open without audiovisual support, and close without audiovisual support. Let the focus be on *you* during these all-important moments. You don't want the audience staring at some screen on the other side of the room. You want—you *deserve*—their full attention.

Some final words of advice about audiovisual support: Be courageous. Consider speaking without using any AV support. I realize this may be heresy in the age of Power Point, but the sad truth is, AV ruins more messages than it helps. The all-too-typical scenario? A speaker says, "Today we're going to talk about quality." And then she flashes a slide that reads, "QUALITY." Now, what does that accomplish? Nothing.

Think about it: When is the last time you heard an audience walk away saying, "Gee, I wish she had more of those word slides!" or "Wow, I really loved all the fine print on his transparencies!" Quite the opposite. Boring slides lead directly to bored audiences. When I have been able to persuade my clients to ditch their slides, invariably they have given their best presentations.

So don't automatically think you need audiovisual support. Most of the time, you'll make a greater impact without it. But if you insist on using AV, at least do it wisely. Prepare for a worst-case scenario. And always take backup—*always.*

"WHAT DID I FORGET?"

A no-fail checklist for audiovisual support:

_____ adapters

_____ plugs

_____ lightbulbs

_____ an extension cord

_____ a roll of heavy-duty tape

_____ pliers

_____ a screwdriver

_____ a flashlight

_____ a fully-charged electronic notebook

_____ a friend with a fully-charged notebook

_____ a complete copy of your presentation on disk

_____ hard-copy backups (All those old-fashioned, low-tech standbys will suddenly look very good if high-tech fails. And trust me on this: High-tech fails an awful lot.)

BODY LANGUAGE

> *"Suit the action to the word and the word to*
> *the action."*
> —WILLIAM SHAKESPEARE, *HAMLET*

Body language isn't something you "glue onto" your message. Instead, good body language will grow naturally out of your material—fitting the occasion and matching your mood. These observations should help:

- Remember Teddy Roosevelt's admonition, "Walk tall and carry a big stick"? Well, I can't vouch for the big stick, but "walk tall" is certainly good advice. **By standing tall and using good posture, you convey confidence.**
- **Gesture naturally, using your full arm and not just your hand.** Merely bending your hand at the wrist looks wishy-washy—a problem that plagued presidential candidate George Bush.
- **Match your gestures to your message.** The best words to focus on? Verbs, because verbs convey action—and action gives you a perfect reason to gesture. EXAMPLES: "Our sales *shot* through the roof"; or, "Now we've got to *slash* expenses." See how moving

your arm up or down can naturally reinforce those messages?

- **Match your gestures to the mood.** In his 1999 State of the Union address, President Clinton showed absolute delight—in words and body language—when both Republicans and Democrats applauded as he proclaimed "equal pay for equal work." With a big grin, Clinton opened his arms wide and then swayed ever so slightly (like a seesaw) from side to side: "That was more encouraging, you know. There was more balance on the seesaw. I like that!"

- Remember: **Hands attract eyes.** The audience will look wherever you put your hands. Don't hide your hands behind your back or bury them in your pockets.

- **Avoid finger counting.** Here is a common mistake: The speaker will talk about "four strategies" and then consecutively hold up one-two-three-four fingers as he presents each strategy. Such movements are simply too small to be effective.

- **Don't point at the audience.** The simple truth is, no one likes to be pointed at.

- **The open hand is a highly effective hand gesture.** Showing the palm of your hand when you speak conveys openness and fosters trust. (This stands in sharp contrast to dismissing listeners with the back of your hand—a negative gesture that distances and alienates.)

- **Avoid making a fist.** After all, what can you do with a fist? Pound on a table? (That looks like a toddler with a temper tantrum.) Punch the air? (That works at a pep rally—but nowhere else.) Heed the Irish proverb, "A closed hand catches no hawk."

- **Stand at a very slight angle to the audience.** When you want to emphasize key points, simply "square" your shoulder (to face the audience). To create drama and make a more powerful impression, you can even move a step or two closer to your listeners.

- **Use appropriate facial expressions to involve the audience:**

    When former U.S. senator Dale Bumpers spoke at the Senate impeachment trial of Bill Clinton, he said the president should have thought more about the consequences of his marital infidelity—"just as Adam and Eve should have, just as *you* and *you* and *you* . . ." Each time he uttered the word "you," Senator Bumpers nodded to the attentive senators. (Lord only knows what the Senators were thinking.)

    When first lady Hillary Rodham Clinton was told she should consider moving to New York and running for U.S. senator, she raised her eyebrows in mock surprise and laughed, "You're kidding!"

- **Beware "lecternitis"**—a serious affliction whereby insecure speakers try to avoid the enemy (also known as the *audience*) by hiding behind defensive artillery (commonly called a *lectern*). A lectern will cover over 75 percent of your body, if you let it. *Don't* let it; try speaking without a lectern. But if you can't quite break the lectern habit yet, at least make an effort to gesture so the audience can see your hands at times. Even better, step to the side of the lectern for the question-and-answer session so they can see your body.

- **Smile.** A smile is the easiest (and cheapest) way to improve your looks—on or off the platform. It's hard to go wrong if you offer your listeners a good smile. They may not always agree with your logic, but they will like you more if you smile when you deliver it.

CLOTHING

> *"Keep up appearances whatever you do."*
> —CHARLES DICKENS

* When Pennsylvania governor Tom Ridge opened the Eighty-first State Farm Show, he wore casual shirt-sleeves to address the 7,600 folks packed in the arena—wisely avoiding suit-and-tie attire in this traditional farm environment.
* When Dr. David Satcher assumed the position of U.S. surgeon general, he received many invitations to speak. An important part of his presentation style? Making it a point to wear the official attire of surgeon general—complete with starched shirt and shiny brass buttons.
* Secretary of State Madeleine Albright has long been known for selecting brooches that complement the message of her speech. Particular favorites? Wearing a red, white, and blue American eagle or a sparkly "Uncle Sam" top hat pin on her overseas trips—proud symbols of U.S. glory.
* At the historic meeting of Yitzhak Rabin and Yasir Arafat on the White House lawn, President Bill Clinton chose to wear a tie with a trumpet pattern—symbolic of the triumph of this day. (Unfortunately, President Clinton does not have an unblemished record in this area. His most inappropriate clothing

display? A news conference addressing the disaster in Bosnia—where he wore a tie with large smiley-faces.)
* Presented with a long day of various speaking engagements, Microsoft chairman Bill Gates changed clothes to match the occasions. He began in a coat and tie; but when he appeared before a large audience on the Stanford campus, he switched to a Stanford sweatshirt. And for a late meeting with reporters? A casual sweater.

My point? Each speaking situation has its own style. Choose clothes that complement the situation. Here are some general tips to consider:

* Avoid fabrics that wrinkle easily. No matter how good they look when you leave home, they won't look attractive after hours of sitting in a car or an airplane, being scrunched by seat belts.
* If you've gained a few pounds, don't try to squeeze into last year's attire. Trust me, you don't need to pop a button as you walk to the lectern. (This actually happened to me a few years ago—and as the button on my dress rolled across the floor in front of my audience, I vowed it would never happen again.)
* If you gesture a lot during presentations, view those gestures in a full-length mirror beforehand. MEN: Pay particular attention to shirt collars that feel too tight. WOMEN: Watch for gaping buttons on your blouse.
* Avoid distracting jewelry. CLUE: If you can't decide whether your jewelry is "distracting" or not—rest assured, it is! Leave it in your jewelry box.

* Empty your pockets of loose change or anything else you might be tempted to fidget with. And don't even think of keeping a ballpoint pen in a pocket. The last thing your presentation needs is nervous pen-clicking.

A final thought about your attire:

* When comedian Garry Shandling was honored by the Museum of Television and Radio, he joked that he wasn't wearing any underwear under his Versace suit. Unless you are a professional comedian, you're probably smart to avoid a quip like that.

COUGHING

> *"What can be the cause of this [coughing] at concerts? I work with literally hundreds of people every day, and I never hear anybody cough. Never. What is there about a concert hall that causes people to disrupt the music?"*
> —GENE SHALIT, FILM CRITIC

Coughing problems fall into two categories: (1) your own coughing spell; or (2) coughing spells in the audience. Both problems are annoying (and frustrating) in their own ways.

Let me start with *your* coughing. If you have a bad cold, ask your physician for recommendations. If you can't cure yourself overnight, have some strategies to keep your coughs at bay—at least for the twenty minutes or so you're standing at the lectern.

Even if you don't have a cold, you should prepare for the possibility of coughing. Always make sure you have a glass of water handy. And always carry a cough drop in your pocket—unwrapped, of course, and preferably broken into small bits so you don't have to talk with an enormous chunk wedged in your jowl. Chances are, you won't need to use the cough drop. But just knowing it's there will boost your comfort level.

Now, about those annoying coughs coming from your audience . . .

* Billy Sunday, the flamboyant evangelist, insisted on total silence when he spoke, period. And if anyone dared to cough, the theatrical preacher would simply stop (mid-sentence, if necessary) and wait for the coughing to end.
* Keith Jarrett, the jazz pianist, once took a brief break in a performance—urging his Montreal audience to get the coughing out of their system once and for all so he could proceed.
* Kurt Masur, conductor of the New York Philharmonic, once literally stopped the orchestra when he heard coughing coming from the audience. And he didn't resume the music until he got the quiet he wanted.
* In Amsterdam, the Concertgebouw symphony hall actually began giving away cough drops to prevent the performers from being annoyed. Whatever works.

EMOTIONS

* During Ronald Reagan's wrap-up of the 1980 campaign, tears came to his eyes when he quoted John Wayne: " 'Give the American people a good cause, and there's nothin' they can't lick.' "

* When Michael Milken pleaded guilty in his big Wall Street insider-trading case, he became emotional with his acknowledgment that "by my acts I have hurt those who are closest to me."
* When Elizabeth Dole announced she would resign her leadership role with the American Red Cross to consider a possible presidential bid, employees sometimes broke into tears.
* When Yitzhak Rabin and Yasir Arafat came together on the White House lawn and exchanged that monumental handshake in the interest of peace in the Middle East, many in the audience cried openly.

Certain occasions trigger emotions—in both the speaker and the audience. Farewells, eulogies, apologies, and resignations are some obvious situations; but even happy occasions tug at the heartstrings: wedding toasts, anniversary tributes, commencement speeches, award ceremonies, baptismal celebrations, bar mitzvahs, to name a few.

The smart speaker plans for emotions. Here are some practical suggestions to ease your delivery:

- **Be realistic.** Admit to yourself that the occasion may trigger tears.
- **Be prepared.** Carry a small handkerchief—clean, white, and folded, please. This is not the occasion for some huge patterned kerchief that you've rolled into a wad. Also, make sure you have a glass of water handy.
- **Plan strategic breaks throughout your presentation.** By pausing after each section, you can prevent an escalating buildup of emotions. An example: I was hired to write a tribute to one of the people who died

in a highly publicized national disaster. Knowing that both the audience and the speaker would be full of emotion, I scripted well-placed pauses into the speech—giving the speaker a chance to sip water, and giving the audience time to collect themselves.

- **Pause the instant you sense tears coming.** A well-timed pause, with a sip of water, might be enough to get you through the emotional passage.

- **Be well-prepared** with a selection of simple, positive statements that can redirect sad emotions. For example, when Elizabeth Dole faced that teary crowd of Red Cross employees, she refocused their attention on the future by saying, "There may be another way for me to serve our country."

- **Consider adjusting the schedule.** If speaking first would be easier, ask to speak first.

- **Consider adjusting the format.** Maybe you could write the tribute, and ask someone else to deliver it on your behalf.

- **Consider taping your message in advance.** You will probably be less emotional if you speak the words in your own home or your own office. Plus, if you are not satisfied with your comments, you have the luxury of retaping. When Rosie O'Donnell arranged for Barbra Streisand to appear on her popular daytime talk show, she specifically chose to tape the program in advance. Why? Because she knew that Streisand's presence would remind her of her mother, who died when Rosie was a child and was a devoted fan of Streisand's music.

- **Know when to quit.** If your tears turn into sobs and you want to stop, you *can* stop. There's no law that says you have to finish. It's your moment, and you can control it in whatever way seems best. When President George Bush gave his tribute to the forty-seven dead crew members of the battleship *Iowa*, he was overwhelmed by emotion. Bush dropped the final lines of his prepared speech, managed to say, "May God bless them," and left.

Keep things in perspective. Tears at the podium are not a crime. If you happen to well up, you aren't committing a federal offense. You are merely showing you're human.

EYE CONTACT

The eye: "The pulse of the soul;
as physicians judge the heart by the pulse,
so we by the eye."
—THOMAS ADAMS

Good eye contact builds rapport, fosters trust, and creates a more likable persona. The simple truth is, we don't like people who can't look us in the eye.

Think about it: What customer would buy a product from a salesperson who hid behind sun glasses? The idea is unthinkable because we rely on eye contact to judge truthfulness. (In fact, eye contact is considered so reliable, that auction bids of thousands of dollars rely exclusively on it.)

The same holds true in everyday conversation. We don't like speakers who can't look us in the eye. We simply wouldn't "buy" an idea from a person who averted his eyes.

Unfortunately, over the years, many speakers have been given bad advice about eye contact. They have been told to "just stare at the back of the room." Mistake! You can't build rapport with a wall.

Instead, I urge my clients to make eye contact with as many *individuals* as possible. Look at one person until you've finished a sentence or made a point—then make eye contact with another person. By focusing on one thought while looking at one person, you will keep on track—and avoid losing your train of thought.

Effective eye contact will:

- build audience rapport
- add variety to your delivery
- reinforce your key points
- improve audience comprehension
- involve listeners from all sections of the room (Although you can't make eye contact with every individual in a big audience, you can certainly acknowledge individuals in each section. By the end of your presentation, you should have scanned the entire room—making everybody feeling included.)

Just as important, this eye contact will *decrease* your nervousness and *increase* your confidence. Why? Because every time you make effective eye contact with a listener, you will *stop* focusing on yourself (the source of all nervousness) and *start* focusing on your listeners (the basis of all good communication).

Eye contact isn't something you just do for your audience. It's something you also do for yourself. Make the most of it.

FORGETTING LINES

Picture this: You're at the lectern, your presentation is going okay, and then you suddenly realize that you forgot to say some key lines—or maybe your mind goes blank and you can't remember what comes next. It feels scary, but there's no reason for panic. You're not alone. This has happened to other speakers—and they've survived.

In 1964, the wonderful singer Robert Goulet was happily singing the National Anthem before the Muhammad Ali–Sonny Liston fight when he suddenly forgot the song's words. His on-the-spot solution? He hummed the rest of his lines.

Humming probably won't rescue the typical speaker, but Robert Goulet's response to the situation offers some inspiration for speakers in similar straits.

* Don't panic.
* Take a brief pause. Sip some water. Look down at your notes.
* No notes? Bet now you wish that you had taken the time to prepare them, huh? Nonetheless, say *something*. Keep it short and simple. Rambling will only put you in a deeper hole.
* Remember: *You* know that you've forgotten your exact lines, but the audience may not realize what's happening—unless you call unnecessary attention to the situation by fumbling and stammering.
* If you can get back on track, great—continue. If not, give a simple summation (repeating your key theme might bail you out), and sit down with as much poise as you can muster.

HANDOUTS

Sarah Wernick, co-author of the best-selling *Strong Women Stay Young* (Bantam Books, 2000), told me two important details about the time she spoke on a panel at a nursing conference: (1) she was the only panelist who offered any handouts; and (2) her presentation was very well received.

I wasn't surprised on either count. Most speakers don't bother preparing handouts. Those who do, generally get good responses. The simple truth is, audiences love handouts. Provide them, and you will likely boost your success. (In fact, conference planners tell me that speakers who provide lots of good handouts typically get higher ratings from the audience on evaluation forms.)

But handouts do present certain delivery problems. For example, if the audience gets the papers beforehand, they'll be reading the material instead of listening to your presentation. In general, you'll be smart to distribute the handouts *after* your presentation. But don't leave your audience hanging. Announce to them that you will be providing copies of all relevant charts, statistics, and reference sources later; otherwise, they'll furiously take notes during the presentation—only to get annoyed later when they find out their copious writing was unnecessary.

One practical suggestion: Be sure to have enough copies. Audiences don't like it when you run out. In fact, make it clear up front that you have more than enough. I once watched an audience literally jump out of their seats to grab a very limited supply of handouts—interrupting the panel so they could get their share of the available copies. Avoid this frenzy at all costs.

A marketing tip: Be sure to include your full address on

each handout so anyone interested can contact you down the road. (You'll be surprised how many people keep handouts for years.)

ONE BIG CAUTION: Never ask audience members to help distribute your handouts. If you happen to ask senior members, they might resent the chore. And if you consciously ask junior members, they might resent being singled out for the lowly task. Do it yourself—or enlist colleagues or volunteers.

HECKLERS

Your chances of having to deal with hecklers are slight. Nonetheless, hecklers do occasionally appear—and when they do, they always present delivery problems.

Hecklers interrupt in a variety of ways. Sometimes with words . . .

* When George Bush was running for president, unionized shipworkers obscured his speech by chanting "Union buster!"
* When Nobel Prize–winning author Elie Wiesel eulogized victims of anti-Semitism in Romania, he was repeatedly interrupted by a woman shouting, "Lies!"

And sometimes a speaker is met with hisses, boos, or jeers . . .

* When Queen Elizabeth II opened a new session of Parliament with the surprising announcement that unelected aristocrats would be stripped of their

centuries-old birthright, she was greeted with unceremonial growls.

* Dr. Louis W. Sullivan, Secretary of Health and Human Services, once had an entire speech was drowned out by the deafening noise of 500 protestors.

Of course, it's highly unlikely that the average speaker will ever be confronted by such extreme events. Nonetheless, it helps to be aware of some possible responses:

* In one of U.S. history's earliest examples of heckling, Patrick Henry was interrupted with cries of "Treason!" when he tried to address the Virginia House of Burgesses. His retort: "If this be treason, make the most of it."
* When Queen Elizabeth II did a walkabout during a visit to New Zealand, she was pelted with eggs. She merely quipped, "I myself prefer my New Zealand eggs for breakfast."
* When Mayor Ed Koch was booed at a farewell tribute to ballerina Patricia McBride, he simply called the booer a "jerk"—and then, in his inimitable fashion, moved directly to the award presentation.
* Geraldine Ferraro used humor when she was heckled at the University of Texas in Arlington—sarcastically thanking the demonstrators for slowing down her rapid-fire New York speaking style.

Perhaps the classiest response of all? Consider this:
The security force automatically intervened when an AIDS activist interrupted New York Governor Mario

Cuomo's State of the State address. But Cuomo specifically requested that security not drag the protestor away. Instead, Cuomo allowed the heckler to remain—and gave him a chance to speak his mind. Cuomo summed up the exchange by telling the legislators, "You can argue with his timing and his taste. You cannot argue with his sincerity."

INTERRUPTIONS

During a meeting at the Bush White House, a presentation was interrupted with a note announcing that another Iraqi SCUD missile had just landed in Israel. You probably won't need to contend with SCUD-missile notices in the middle of your next presentation. But interruptions happen. Here are just a few that I have personally experienced:

- **fire alarms**

I once heard alarms interrupt a professional conference where over a thousand attendees had gathered in the hotel ballroom. Fortunately, the speaker, sociolinguist Deborah Tannen, was unruffled—and graciously offered to stay longer to compensate for the lost time. A wise lesson for any speaker: Always know where the nearest exits are, and be able to offer clear directions if evacuation is necessary.

- **pagers, beepers, cell phones**

No one is immune to these annoyances—it even happened at a White House state dinner. As President Clinton offered a toast to Argentine president Carlos Menem, the ring of a cell phone punctuated the air. Personally, I'd like to see laws against noisy cell phones. Until then, a few firm glances of disgust should do the trick.

- **opening and closing doors**

You can prevent these unnecessary interruptions simply by posting the name of your meeting on the outside of *every* door leading into your room. For extra assurance, ask colleagues to position themselves in the hallway, to intercept interlopers before they can do damage.

- **waiters dropping dishes**

Sorry, there's not a whole lot you can do about this one unless you wait until the tables are cleared before speaking—which may cause your meeting to run late.

- **announcements from public-address systems**

This is a routine problem if you're talking to students in a public school, where half of the learning day seems to be interrupted by P.A. announcements. You just have to roll with it. Use the "free time" to drink some water or gather materials.

- **crying babies**

When a wailing baby interrupted a Peter, Paul and Mary concert, singer Peter Yarrow smiled, grew silent, and then quipped about the baby's "harmony."

- **disruptive children**

Common sense can prevent some of these problems.

What's the sense in starting a community meeting at eight P.M.? Begin earlier, so families can leave before their tired kids get too restless.

Lyndon Johnson did not cotton to interruptions during his speeches—particularly interruptions from children. His technique? Stop the speech, glare at the child, and then order the mother to correct the matter immediately. (A technique not for the fainthearted, I might add.)

MICROPHONES

When you decide to use sound amplification, you have two choices. You can either (1) use the microphone properly and build a closer connection to the audience; or (2) bungle the microphone and annoy your audience. The choice is entirely yours.

Stack the deck in your favor by asking:

- **Do I need to use a sound system at all?**

If everyone can hear you without amplification, for heaven's sake, forgo the mike! Don't use a sound system for a small group, or in a room with excellent accoustics—that only distances you from the audience. The easiest way to test your audibility? Do a test beforehand. Simply ask some listeners in the back if they can hear you. If they seem comfortable nodding yes, then move ahead on your own steam. But if they respond with puzzled stares or bewildered faces, use a mike.

- **How can I check out the sound system?**

You have a right to expect professional assistance. Ask to meet the sound engineer. Be exceedingly nice to this person. If the sound engineer likes you, he is more likely to stay around and be ready to step in and help if you run into any problems. (If the sound engineer leaves the area, be sure you know how to reach him in a hurry!)

- **How should I test the microphone?**

Just talk into it normally, and have someone listen. Don't tap it. Don't blow into it. Talk normally. Of course, that raises a question: What should you say during your test? Well, "testing, one-two-three" will do the job. But in the 1988 Bush-Dukakis debate, Massachusetts governor Michael

Dukakis used his microphone check as a relaxation technique—rhythmically reeling off the names of the Boston Red Sox players who had played on the team when he saw his first Red Sox game at age four.

A NOTE OF CAUTION: During a voice test, President Reagan once made a quip about the "bunch of no-good lousy bums" in the Polish military—not realizing that the sound was already on. The moral? Don't say anything you don't want people to overhear.

- **What can I learn from listening to the other speakers?**

A lot. Listen to how well the sound system works for the speakers who are ahead of you. Make adjustments as necessary.

- **Should I use a handheld mike or a clip-on mike?**

Some people prefer a handheld mike because it gives them something to do with their hands. Others (me included) prefer a lavalier (or clip-on) microphone because we like having our hands free to gesture.

  * Three cautions regarding handheld mikes: (1) Handle the mike carefully to avoid unwanted noises. Your audience really does not want to hear amplification of clunking rings or jangling bracelets. (2) Don't put it too close to your mouth, otherwise you'll have distortion. Simply point the mike toward your mouth from a distance of six to eight inches—and let the mike do the rest of the work. (3) Remember to move the mike with you as you turn your head.

  * Two cautions regarding clip-on mikes: (1) Be sure your outfit is suitable for attaching the mike. I once wore a plain-front dress to an important speaking engagement—only to find there was no place to

secure the available mike. (2) Clip-ons are more fragile and more prone to feedback. Have a sound engineer nearby.

- **How should I use a microphone that's attached to the lectern?**

Check the lectern's height. You don't want to be forced to stretch or stoop. (Bending downward into the mike affects the pitch of your voice and interferes with eye contact.) Adjust the microphone's position before you speak, and once it's set, *don't touch that mike* unless it's absolutely necessary. (If you do, you risk subjecting the audience to a series of metallic groans.) Stay at a constant distance from the mike to prevent vocal fading. *Relax*—there's no need to stand like a statue in front of the mouthpiece. You can move a bit, as long as you speak *toward* the microphone.

- **Are multiple microphones involved?**

Be aware of the potential for serious feedback problems with more than one microphone— perhaps for panelists at a head table, or in the audience for a Q&A.

- **What should I do if the microphone produces feedback?**

Call upon that engineer—quickly. The microphone failed when Elizabeth Dole gave her terrific speech at the Republican National Convention, and a well-prepared assistant speedily handed her another mike. In some rooms, you can go accoustic. Your voice might not be as loud as you'd like, but at least it will sound better than that horrendous mechanical screeching.

A final thought about things that can go wrong with microphones:

Governor Mario Cuomo and Senator Alfonse D'Amato

both appeared at an annual meeting of the Association of Towns of the State of New York. Two prominent men, two firm opinions, two strong personalities—and one mike. Add it up, and the audience got a verbal sparring match. As the governor spoke, the senator actually marched up to the microphone and interrupted Cuomo's speech. Within moments, the audience got to see a once-in-a-lifetime spectacle—a prominent governor holding his mike, and a prominent senator trying to grab it away.

I'm not sure what lesson you can learn from this, but hold your microphone tight, and keep a sharp eye out for interlopers.

Misspeaking

It happens a lot. You mean to say one thing . . . but a slip of the tongue brings something else out of your mouth.

* Campaigning for the presidency, Massachusetts governor Michael Dukakis referred to "modern musicians" instead of "modern munitions."
* Jimmy Carter once referred to himself as a "former president"—while still in office. (I believe psychiatrists could have had a field day with that one.)
* Dan Quayle's frequent flubs became grist for the comedy mill. In one of his more memorable utterances, Quayle took the motto of the United Negro College fund ("A mind is a terrible thing to waste") and somehow managed to come out with this: "What a waste it is to lose one's mind or not to have a mind. How true that is."
* President George Bush once shocked an American Legion audience by referring to September 7 as Pearl

Harbor day (which is actually *December* 7). One year later he told another American Legion audience that he would never make the mistake again: "As long as I live, I'll remember the gasps from the audience." Alas, Bush then misspoke in this speech and referred to December 7 as "election day."

* President Ronald Reagan, "the Great Communicator," made frequent flubs, but used his charm to gloss over them. He might refer to the Vienna airport as the Vietnam airport, or assign the wrong title to Mikhail Gorbachev.

My point is, flubs happen—a lot, even to the best speakers. You are not immune. If you botch your material, correct yourself simply and calmly. Try a brief, neutral statement, such as:

* "Let me try that one more time."
* "Actually, the date is . . ."
* "I should clarify that."
* "Let me correct that."
* "What I really meant to say was . . ."
* "Maybe I should put it another way."
* "I need to fix that. The correct number is . . ."

Keep your correction short and clean. Don't stammer—otherwise, you'll just call more attention to your error. Elaborate apologies only dig deeper holes. If you are comfortable with humor, a lighthearted line might help.

* "Can we do a retake on that?"
* "How about if I give you an instant replay?"

* "Now, for those of you who lack fluency in garble, let me translate that into plain, ordinary English."
* "Well, I sure mangled that one, didn't I?"
* "Gee, it might help if I took my foot out of my mouth!"

My all-time favorite flub? Vice President Bush was describing his close relationship with President Reagan when he got a bit carried away. Emphasizing the seven and a half years they'd worked side by side, Bush said, "We have had triumphs, we have made mistakes, we have had sex." Pause—stunned silence. The vice president quickly corrected his last line ("We have had *setbacks*"), and drew hearty laughter from the audience. Bush's perfect ad-lib? "I feel like a javelin thrower who won the coin toss and elected to receive."

NOTES AND MANUSCRIPTS

As a speaker, you have three delivery options:

(1) Speak without any notes.
(2) Use notes (or an outline).
(3) Use a full manuscript—with every word written down.

Only you can decide the best delivery option for your particular speaking situation. Consider all the factors to make an intelligent decision.

* **Speaking without notes**
  * When Hillary Clinton appeared on Capitol Hill before the House Ways and Means Committee, she

impressed observers by not using notes—and speaking with confidence, grace, and clarity.

* When Mikhail Gorbachev gave a series of speeches to U.S. business groups, he likewise impressed executives by not using notes—and speaking knowledgeably about complex economic issues.

If you are a highly accomplished speaker, you will make a strong impression with the "no notes" option. Audiences will surely appreciate your grasp of the material. However, few speakers can pass the "no notes" test. And few want to try.

If you've ever lost your train of thought in front of an audience (or if you've ever rambled and run overtime), you'll appreciate the importance of having some written material to support your message. And if you've ever witnessed a speaker without notes stumble at the lectern, you'll be inspired to avoid that pitfall yourself.

When presidential candidate Bob Dole gave rehearsed speeches on education reform, he made a terrific impact. But when he appeared at an unscripted forum to discuss the same topic, he dug a hole for himself.

If you're tempted to take the "no notes" option, make sure you have the necessary delivery skills. Remember: You never get the second chance to give a speech.

• using notes

You can either prepare a formal outline on standard-size white copy paper (8½ × 11 inches) . . . or put "bullet point" notes on simple index cards. The choice is yours. No matter how you choose to prepare your notes, consider these guidelines:

* Use a large typeface (or neatly print in large hand-writing).
* Allow wide margins. Do not squish material close together. Why? Because if you want to add some last-minute points (as often happens), the extra space will be useful.
* Number each page or each index card. (Believe me: If you accidentally drop your notes on the way to the lectern, you'll be very grateful to have everything numbered in correct order.)
* Do not staple the pages or index cards together. That would require awkward flipping at the lectern. Instead, a paper clip will hold all the sheets in their proper order—and let you easily slide from one piece of paper to the next.
* Underline any important statistics so you can spot them at a glance.
* Use colored pencils or yellow highlighters to emphasize key points.
* Draw clear lines across the page to separate the major sections of your presentation.
* Carefully time your entire presentation. Too many folks look at their outline and assume it will take about fifteen minutes to deliver. Unfortunately, the outline reflects only the "skeleton" of their presentation. When they start adding unrehearsed details at the lectern, they learn (the hard way) that their message runs too long.

WARNING: Don't skimp on the thought process that goes into a good outline. Learn from experienced speakers, who often discipline themselves to write their entire presentation first—and then work backwards, later reducing their manuscript to abbreviated notes.

• using a full manuscript

Why should you go to all the work of preparing a full manuscript for your speech? Wouldn't it be easier to "wing it"?

Well, let me answer this way: The CEOs of top corporations pay freelance speechwriters $3,000–$7,000 (and more) to write a speech. They wouldn't repeatedly pay for those manuscripts unless they saw substantial returns on their investment.

The truth is, a well-written speech manuscript packs a powerful punch. You can count on these important advantages:

• a guaranteed time frame

You'll never have to worry about running overtime again. Want to judge the length of a manuscript speech? It's as easy as one-two-three.

(1) Use your computer to get the total number of words in your manuscript.

(2) Divide by your rate of speaking. (The average person talks about 120–150 words per minute.)

(3) You'll get a good estimate—but time your remarks carefully when you rehearse so you're as accurate as possible.

• a clear and focused message

Manuscripts prevent rambling—and make a stronger impression.

• thoroughness

Is there anything worse than sitting down after a speech and realizing you forgot to say your most important point?

- **ease of delivery**

  Indeed, having a manuscript might do more to calm your pre-speech jitters than anything else. After all, you won't lose sleep worrying about "going blank" at the podium.

- **accuracy**

  Avoid fumbled statistics. Making his first impression as the new U.S. delegate to the United Nations, William Richardson botched his numbers, saying the UN had 148 members instead of 185. Such errors are common—and preventable with a good manuscript.

- **precise, powerful wording**

  People praised President Ronald Reagan as "the Great Communicator," but that skill was apparent only when he used carefully scripted manuscripts. Without notes, Reagan often misspoke.

- **subtle nuances**

  Avoid poorly chosen words to prevent accidental meanings.

- **flexibility**

  Remember: You still have the option of adding extemporaneous comments. There's no law that says you have to stick with your manuscript word for word. Skilled speakers regularly make last-minute comments to add spontaneity

- **a professional appearance**

  Let's face it—influential people hire speechwriters to gain advantage in communicating. You can rely on a well-written manuscript to gain that same advantage.

- **greater credibility**

  A manuscript conveys authority. An audience will see that you did your homework.

- **appropriate humor**

  You will avoid off-the-cuff jokes that might hurt your career or alienate the audience.

- **practicality**

  You get hit with the flu, or with a last-minute emergency. Does this mean you must cancel a scheduled speaking engagement? Not necessarily. With a good manuscript, a colleague could step in and deliver your message.

- **long-lasting publicity**

  If you give copies of your remarks to the audience, you can extend the life of your message.

Do you need any more good reasons to invest the time to create a well-crafted manuscript? Well, here's one other reason—and it might prove to be the most important:

You can distribute copies of your manuscript to the press and get valuable media coverage. A speech originally given to a room of twenty people might wind up quoted in the press—extending your message to thousands, or even millions. Case in point:

Charles Francis, owner of the IdeaBank online research service, was invited to address a professional association in New York City. The clever title of his speech? *How to Stop Boring Your Audience to Death.* Unfortunately, a snowstorm struck, and only a handful of us showed up to hear his lively message. But this experienced speaker made the most of the situation. Afterward, he wisely sent his manuscript to *Vital Speeches of the Day*, which reprinted the speech in their prestigious publication—dramatically increasing the size of his audience. Now, that's the power of a good manuscript speech!

WHATEVER YOU DO . . . whether you prefer notes or manuscripts, don't forget to take them. Written materials won't do you much good if you leave them sitting back on your kitchen table. Don't laugh. It happens. After more than a quarter of a century in jail, Nelson Mandela momentously emerged a free man. But when he went to give the speech he had written for this momentous occasion in Capetown, he realized he had left his reading glasses and his manuscript back in the jail.

And then there's the sad story of a vice admiral in England. Ready to speak to the Royal Navy Old Comrades Association, he looked at his notes—only to discover that he had accidentally brought his wife's shopping list instead.

You see: It's a moot point whether you use notes or a full manuscript—if you forget to bring them to the presentation! In fact, bring two sets. This becomes especially important when you're checking luggage at airports. You don't want to leave the only copy of your notes in luggage.

A personal note here:

Shortly after my first book was published (*How to Write and Give a Speech*, St. Martin's Press, 1984), I received a very nice letter from a reader. Apparently, after reading my book, she had followed my suggestion and made an extra copy of her next presentation. Sure enough, the luggage containing her speech was lost en route—and without the duplicate copy she had wisely carried in her briefcase, her well-planned presentation would have gone down the tubes.

I don't remember that reader's name, but I'm glad my suggestion helped her, and I'd like to thank her for taking the time to write and share her experience. Here's hoping this advice will prevent problems for you, as well.

NERVOUSNESS

> *"Nothin' wrong with your knees shakin'. When I*
> *first shook, it was half nervousness, half movin' to*
> *the beat . . . and look what it did for me."*
> —ELVIS

Stage fright. Butterflies. The jitters. A bad case of the nerves. No matter what you call it, it doesn't feel good. On that historic day when Yitzhak Rabin and Yasir Arafat were to meet on the South Lawn of the White House, President Clinton was so worried about the speech he would make, that he woke up at three A.M. and couldn't fall back to sleep.

Former New York governor Mario Cuomo, surely recognized as one of the best speakers in the country, admits that giving speeches is never easy. "You hope they'll call up and say they have to cancel." Actually, that's a common fantasy for speakers. They often wish the event will "just go away." (It doesn't.)

* When invited to give the commencement address at my alma mater, the College of William and Mary, actress Glenn Close got a case of the jitters—and secretly hoped the whole event would just disappear. Of course, she went on to deliver a terrific speech.
* Winston Churchill once felt so nervous that he fainted in front of the audience.
* Barbara Bush used to be so shy and insecure that she actually cried at the mere thought of having to speak to the Houston Garden Club.
* Audrey Hepburn, who thrilled movie audiences for decades, never spoke in public until she became an

ambassador for UNICEF. Her reaction to her new-found public speaking role? "It scares the wits out of me."

So the question is: If some of the most polished, most successful, most beloved personalities in the world get nervous about presenting in public—what hope can the rest of us have?

Well, truth be told, everyone gets nervous before speaking. It's just that some people learn to do a better job of handling the situation.

Good advice comes from accomplished speaker Jack Valenti, president of the Motion Picture Association of America. According to Valenti, "the most effective antidote to stage fright and other calamities of speechmaking is total, slavish, monkish preparation." And he's right. Preparation will do more than anything else to prevent nervousness.

I travel all around the country, speaking to professional organizations. Many people admit they don't feel confident about their speaking skills—and yet when I ask about their preparation tactics, they confess they frequently wing it.

Well, "winging it" is the surest road to feeling nervous! Good preparation will do more to boost your confidence level than anything else. So, start there. Prepare—every time. But be realistic. Even the best-prepared speakers can experience nervousness. If that happens to you, the following tips may be lifesavers.

- **before you speak**
  * Take care of basic needs. Use the bathroom. Make sure you have a handkerchief handy. Pour a glass of water to place at the lectern. (No ice, please. You

don't want to be choking on a cube up there.) Unwrap a cough drop so it's ready to use. If you suffer from dry mouth, put a thin layer of Vaseline ointment on your teeth so your lips won't get stuck.

* Focused movement will help burn nervous energy. Find practical ways to move your body. Go to a drinking fountain. Walk down the hall. Go to the back of the room to look at some materials. Shut a door. Adjust a window shade. Get your business cards ready so you don't have to fumble for them after your presentation. (CAUTION: Avoid *un*focused movement, such as pacing or repeatedly shuffling papers. Such restlessness will only increase your nervousness—and create a negative impression.)

* Stuck at your seat? Look for simple opportunities that will create purposeful movement. Put your pen in your briefcase. Hand something to an associate. Adjust your posture. Uncross your legs. Sit up straighter. Sip the cup of tea you wisely brought along (great for relaxing your vocal cords as well as easing your nervousness). Reach for a notepad. Take some notes. Even small movements can help dissipate nervousness—and give you a sense of being in control.

* Think positive. Make affirming statements to yourself: "I really know my subject. . . . These people respect me. . . . I can give a lot of helpful information today. . . . I've been preparing for weeks. . . . Audiences give me good evaluations. . . ."

* Breathe. Deeply and slowly.

* Put psychologist William James to the test. It was James who first described the "as if" principle: Act *as*

if you are confident, and you truly will become confident. A great deal of psychological theory goes into this, but to put it in a nutshell: Your body tends to do what your mind expects. If your mind expects a successful presentation, your body is more likely to produce one.

* Dr. Norman Vincent Peale, author of *The Power of Positive Thinking*, offered this: "It is my practice before making a speech to pray for the people present and to send out thoughts of love and good will toward them." (Dr. Peale was shy and insecure as a young speaker. He later credited "positive thinking" for his platform success.)

* Avoid negative thoughts like the plague. The minute you find yourself thinking, "I know I'm going to get nervous," you must stop that thought immediately. Replace it with a positive affirmation: "This is a popular topic. The audience will like hearing about it." Can't manage anything positive? Then mentally recite something like a grocery list. It may not be profound, but at least it's better than something negative.

* Avoid negative people. If a coworker grates on your nerves, walk away. Can't think of a gracious escape? Go to the bathroom and lock yourself in a stall. It's better than being flustered by a colleague.

• **in the opening moments**

Speakers typically feel most nervous at the very beginning. Here are a few suggestions for quelling the jitters:

* Make your opening lines clear and crisp; know them inside out. The more confident you sound, the less nervous you will feel.

* Speak a bit louder than usual. The trick for getting better volume? Direct your speech to the back row.
* Use gestures to burn off your nervous energy. (Check the "Body Language" section for more details.)
* Make strategic eye contact. Overcome the common tendency of looking at someone sitting close to you. Instead, direct your opening lines to someone in the back of the room. (Check the "Eye Contact" section for more details.)
* Breathe. Aren't you glad you cleverly built some pauses into your presentation? The perfect chance to take a breath. . . .

- **common problems**
  * dry mouth.

    Sip some water. Forgot to take a glass to the podium? Bet you won't forget again! But, in a pinch, lightly chew your tongue. Soon you'll have saliva.
  * shaking hands

    Make a bold gesture to dissipate the energy. Use your whole arm. Whatever you do, *don't* hold anything in your hands! A quivery pointer or rattling papers will only draw attention to your nervousness.
  * pounding heart

    Relax. They can't see or hear your heartbeat—in spite of the fact that it probably sounds like a big cannon to you.
  * sweaty palms

    Only you will know. Keep plowing ahead.
- **after your presentation**
  * Maintain a professional presence. Yes, you can relax a bit after you leave the podium. But no, you can't

totally "kick back." Remember: The audience will still be looking at you.

* Resist the tendency to start chatting. Pay attention to other speakers—or at least be quiet and look like you're paying attention.

* Above all, learn from your experience. May I suggest a post-presentation critique?

This information will help you identify the times when you're most susceptible to nervousness.

"WHEN DID I FEEL THE MOST NERVOUS?"

I felt most nervous at the following times:

_____ when I first got the assignment

_____ when I began the preparation

_____ when I found out how large the audience was

_____ when I did my first rehearsal

_____ when I learned who would introduce me

_____ the week before

_____ the day before

_____ the night before

_____ the morning of the speech

_____ as I was being introduced

_____ as I was walking to the lectern

_____ as I said my opening lines

_____ when I recognized friends/relatives in the audience

_____ in the middle

_____ at the end

_____ when someone in the audience gave me an unfriendly look

_____ when someone in the audience fell asleep

_____ when there was an interruption
_____ during the Q&A
_____ at the networking session afterward

PAUSES

"That impressive, eloquent, progressive silence which often achieves a desired effect where no combination of words howsoever felicitous could accomplish it."
—MARK TWAIN

The late Jack Benny, that master comedian, didn't have to say a word to get a laugh. He could break up any crowd with a well-timed pause. Most speakers don't need to use pauses so dramatically. But smart speakers always know how to use pauses effectively.

Where can you pause?

- **after introductory phrases or clauses**
  * "By the time we finish with these endless meetings [PAUSE], we may have a whole new set of problems."
  * "Even though the School Board meeting went well, [PAUSE] the teachers still feel uneasy."
- **before conjunctions** (*but, or, and, because*, et cetera)
  * "We strongly urged them to revise the proposal [PAUSE], but they didn't listen to our advice."
  * "We must include it in the budget *this* year [PAUSE], or face serious consequences *next* year."
- **when running down a long list of items**
  * "We'll need to call the vendors [PAUSE], double-check our contracts [PAUSE], verify all details [PAUSE], con-

firm the agenda [PAUSE], and allow time to make adjustments."

- **when you want to create audience interest**
  - * "Maybe you wonder if this will affect you. [PAUSE] It will. [PAUSE] Hard. [PAUSE] Right in the pocketbook."
- **whenever you need to take a brief break**
  - * to sip some water
  - * to pop a cough drop
  - * to adjust your papers
  - * to take a breath
- **whenever emotions overcome you, and you need to collect yourself**

Senator Edward Kennedy spoke at American University in Washington, D.C., to commemorate a major address given there almost three decades earlier by his brother, President John F. Kennedy. The senator's delivery was smooth until he began to reminisce about his late brother. He became emotional and then simply stopped speaking—pausing a long time before he could continue.

- **whenever an interruption distracts the audience's attention—or your concentration**

Surprised by an unwelcome interruption? Rather than look flustered, simply pause—and give yourself time to collect your thoughts.

PROOFREADING

Proofread all your materials: your slides, your handouts, your manuscript. Mistakes can cause an audience to question your professionalism and doubt your credibility.

Typos can also hurt your delivery. How? If you accidentally read a typo from your notes (say, "this venereal institution" instead of "this venerable institution"), you will look flustered as you make an awkward correction.

PROOFREADING GUIDELINES

Use this proofreading checklist for your next presentation.

_____ Increase the size of your type and also use double-spacing when you proofread. The larger typeface will make typos stand out, and the extra white space will give you room for making notes.

_____ Begin by reading aloud. It helps to "hear" your mistakes.

_____ Silently read each page backward—from the last line on the page up to the first. This prevents you from anticipating words. By focusing on what is actually written, you will be more likely to catch "missing" words. (Food for thought: What if Moses had omitted the word not from the Ten Commandments?)

_____ Juxtapose pages. This lets you analyze each page as a unit—and prevents you from being distracted by the overall meaning. (Just make sure each page is numbered.)

_____ Vary your routine. Work at different times and in different locations.

_____ Get friendly with a nitpicker. Every office, every school, every family, has at least one person who lives to catch other people's mistakes. Do not get annoyed with these nitpickers—get friendly, real friendly. Invite these fine folks to a proofreading party. Buy them coffee. Put boxes of donuts on the table. Encourage them to linger and nitpick to their hearts' content. They will enjoy feeling superior each time they catch a mistake—and you will enjoy having clean, coherent copy.

_____ With two proofreaders, have each partner start at opposite ends of the material. The simple truth is: People get tired toward the end of reading, and miss errors.

_____ Build a good reference library. Refer to the experts whenever you are in doubt about usage.

_____ Get phone numbers or websites for "grammar hotlines." (Some colleges and universities maintain phone lines to handle grammar questions. Inquire in your area.)

_____ When you find a mistake, take another look. Typos tend to come in clusters.

_____ Pay special attention to common "danger spots":
* numbered lists

It's embarrassing to admit, but I once gave a speech that botched this basic rule. As a result of some hasty, on-site editing, I wound up with a list that included two "number 4's" and no "number 5." That sorry incident took place almost two decades ago, but I still remember the lesson: If you fiddle with a numbered list in any way, double-check the order.
* alphabetical lists

If you make this mistake on a slide, it will stand out like a sore thumb.
* the beginning of a paragraph

* the last word on a line
* a new section
* changes in typeface
* missing double quote marks

It's especially dangerous to miss the second quotation mark. Why? Because an unaware speaker may not realize when the actual quotation ends.

* small print
* "boilerplate"

Don't gloss over "throwaway" sections. You can never be sure what's in them unless you read them carefully.

* abbreviations

Do you want to say "U.S.A." or "the United States of America"?

* statistics

Beware inversions. There's a big difference between *$12* million and *$21* million. Make sure you catch this typo before your audience does.

* proper names

Try to keep an entire name on one line. Avoid a line break between the first and last names. Double-check spellings and phonetic pronunciations.

* broken sentences

Do not carry a sentence from one page to the next. It's too easy for a speaker to get lost midway.

* trademarks

Always capitalize registered trademarks, and use them as adjectives with the generic term for that product. For example: "Baggies plastic bags," "Kool-Aid soft-drink mix," or "Frigidaire appliances." If you don't want to use the trademark, then just use the generic product terms—"facial tissues" (instead of "Kleenex") or "copiers" (instead of "Xerox machines"). But, whatever you do, don't use a trademark without the generic name. WRONG: "So then I told her to xerox it." RIGHT: "So then I told her to copy it."

* page numbers

Here's a speaker's nightmare: Because of a photocopying error, the final manuscript contained two copies of page 3. The speaker began to read page 3 twice—and wondered why the audience looked puzzled!

* revised sections

Even if you changed only one word, you must re-proofread the entire section. Typos have a funny way of slipping in.

_____ Ask yourself, "What mistake would do the most harm?" Misspelling your boss's name? Mispronouncing the name of your biggest contributor? Inverting the financial figures on an important chart? Omitting the credits for prominent executives? Double-check important data. And when you're done, *triple*-check it.

In proofreading, a touch of paranoia can prove to be a career asset. After all, you don't want to wind up in front of an audience with a chart that reads, *Strategies to Overcome Literacy*—as I once saw someone do at a meeting.

And you certainly don't want to leave out the *l* in a

prominent headline about "Public Relations"—as I once had the distinction of doing myself. (Only a few colleagues remember the "Pubic Relations" fiasco from my distant editorial past—and when they read this, I have no doubt they will take great glee in calling me on it.)

PROPS

Props give audiences something to look at, something to reinforce the message, and something to remember. Props also give the media something to photograph for visual appeal.

Just as important, props give speakers something concrete to do with their hands—a terrific plus for burning up nervous energy. The possibilities are almost endless:

* When New Jersey governor Christine Whitman spoke about ending the sales tax on long-distance calls, she dramatized the situation by placing a phone call in the middle of her speech.
* White House counsel Charles Ruff dramatically displayed a pocket-sized copy of the U.S. Constitution when he opened President Clinton's impeachment defense.
* During the memorial for the Columbine High School massacre in 1999, Colorado governor Bill Owens read the name of each of the thirteen victims—as a white dove fluttered into the sky for each person.
* In his first televised budget speech, President Ronald Reagan scored points by using a handful of small change to show the value of the dollar.

* When St. Louis Rams coach Dick Vermeil announced his retirement (just two days after winning his first Super Bowl), he was flanked by symbols of his football career: on one side, his Super Bowl trophy . . . and on the other side, a wheelbarrow, representing Vermeil's dedication to hard work.

* Speakers from MADD (Mothers Against Drunk Driving) regularly try to personalize the issue of drunken driving. One effective technique: Sharing photos of loved ones who died at the hands of a drunk driver . . . or holding up a football jersey that was worn by the victim.

* A Woman's Place, an organization devoted to the victims of domestic violence, holds a candlelight vigil each year at the Bucks County (PA) Courthouse. The ceremony includes "An Empty Place at the Table" display—with table settings provided by the victims' loved ones.

* Many years ago, I attended a dynamic presentation by Jack Felton, who was in charge of public relations for McCormick Foods. Jack's topic? The need to look at everything with fresh eyes. His prop: a deck of playing cards printed with the suits in the wrong color—with black and red switched. I still have his red ace pinned to my office bulletin board, and every time I see that playing card, I remember Jack's terrific message.

* One speaker used clothing as a prop—wearing a leisure suit from the 1970s. His point? "We would look pretty foolish if we still dressed the way we did twenty-five years ago. But yet, how many times do we still think the same old way?"

* One fund-raiser launched his campaign by pulling a $20 bill out of his pocket and plunking it on the lectern—starting the collection right there.
* Inexpensive options: key chains with clever slogans . . . fortune cookies with corporate messages . . . pencils with motivational mottoes . . . balloons with printed sales logos . . .

Be creative with props. Your audience will welcome your efforts.

REHEARSALS

Activist Abbie Hoffman used to practice his speeches for the college lecture circuit by shouting out the window to a pair of llamas grazing in a nearby field. Of course, your rehearsals don't have to be quite that dramatic.

You can rehearse at the office, at home, in the car, or even in a hammock. (President Clinton liked to practice his State of the Union speeches at the kitchen table.) *Where* you rehearse doesn't make much difference. The important thing is: *Do it.*

Tempted to skip your practice sessions? *Don't.* Learn from the ancient Greek orator Demonsthenes. Demonsthenes shaved one side of his head so he would be too embarrassed to go out in public—thereby ensuring he would stay inside and practice his oratory.

Okay, you probably don't need to take such radical steps. Nonetheless, you still need to exercise discipline if you're going to say something that sounds good. Try this simple progression:

(1) Begin by just reading your speech aloud—sitting down, if that makes you more comfortable. Feel free to stop as often as you want to make minor edits or add delivery notes.

(2) Then practice the presentation from beginning to end without stopping so you can time it accurately. Do not allow yourself to repeat sections. If you make a mistake, fix it exactly the way you would in front of an audience—with no back-tracking.

(3) Next, record your speech into a tape recorder. Get familiar with the content by listening to the tape. This is an easy way to "rehearse" while you're busy commuting or jogging. You can also use the tape to time various sections of your speech.

(4) Now deliver it once or twice standing up, so you get a chance to use gestures. See how you look in a full-length mirror, if possible.

(5) Invite a trusted colleague or a spouse to watch a run-through. (If this rehearsal does not go well, relax. You still have time to make improvements. Do *not* emulate Arturo Toscanini, the famed conductor of the Metropolitan Opera in New York. If things went badly during rehearsal, Toscanini supposedly threw the expensive score at the orchestra—not a productive habit for most speakers.)

(6) If possible, practice at least once in the actual presentation room. Adjust your voice to match the size of the room.

(7) Try presenting to a group of coworkers just to get a

feel for an audience. (CAUTION: Do not invite co-workers with passive-aggressive personalities or obsessive-compulsive tendencies. They will either deflate your spirits, or pick your presentation to shreds. Keep them as far away as possible.)

(8) Consider hiring a professional speech coach—particularly if you will be a featured speaker at a major event. (Section seven gives practical advice on hiring a coach.)

(9) Pay special attention to any technical needs—microphone, slide support, video clips. Don't assume your slides will work the way they did in your office. Don't assume the microphone is properly adjusted. Practice *everything*. Leave *nothing* to chance.

(10) Pay special attention to any delivery problems you may have had in the past. Throughout this rehearsal process, review the self-evaluations presented in Section Seven. By looking at past delivery mistakes, you can prevent future problems.

Good rehearsal advice comes from Harvey Mackay, popular speaker and bestselling author of *Beware the Naked Man Who Offers You His Shirt* (Fawcett). Mackay says, "I believe in continuous improvement, and to achieve it you must get constant, immediate, unfiltered feedback from your audience. For the past twenty-five years, I've been telling people to pick up the phone and call Toastmasters." For more information about Toastmasters and other helpful organizations for speakers, turn to the appendix in Section Eight.

Whatever you do, *learn* from your rehearsals. With each

run-through, your delivery should improve—and your confidence will increase.

VOICE

"Speak clearly, if you speak at all; carve every word before you let it fall."
—OLIVER WENDELL HOLMES

You do not have to hire a professional coach to improve the quality of your voice. A few simple observations will point you in the right direction for some valuable self-improvement.

You can get started with this simple test. There are no "right" or "wrong" answers. Just answer as honestly as possible, so you understand the connection between your voice and your personality.

MY VOCAL PERSONALITY

(1) Am I comfortable with the sound of my own voice?

(2) Has anyone ever commented about the quality of my voice—either with praise or criticism? What was the underlying motivation for those comments?

(3) How does my voice compare with my parents' voices? With my siblings'? (NOTE: Just as each family has a genetic makeup, each family also has a vocal makeup. Think about the relatives you grew up with. Did they yell? Whisper? Whine? Intimidate? How are your voices similar? How do they differ?)

(4) How does my voice reflect my personality?

(5) Is there any part of my personality I would like to change? If so, how would a different voice reflect that?

(6) How does my voice reflect my health status? How does my voice change when I'm sick? . . . tired? . . . hungry? . . . have a headache?

(7) How does my voice reflect my emotional status? How do I sound when I'm worried? . . . sad? . . . frustrated? . . . angry?

(8) In social settings, does my voice make people feel comfortable? You don't have to be a genius to figure this out. Simply observe the way people react when you talk. Maybe people physically back away from you because you talk too loudly. Or maybe they have a puzzled look on their faces because you mumble. Take stock of how your voice is received by others.

(9) In business settings, does my voice convey authority? Again, simply observe what happens in meetings. Do colleagues interrupt because your ideas seem weak? . . . finish your sentences because you're so long-winded? . . . avoid eye contact because they don't like you? . . . make you repeat things because you talk too softly?

(10) Do I match my voice to express my message? Serious messages need a serious voice. For example: Don't ask a colleague about the status of a major report in the same tone you'd use to ask your child about lunch.

(11) Do I match my voice to fit the situation? Think, for

a moment, about all the places where you must talk in the course of a day. Is your breakfast-table voice the same as your job-interview voice? Is your elevator voice as loud as your cafeteria voice? Is your car-pool voice the same as your basketball-league voice? If so, you might be alienating a lot of listeners.

(12) Do I adjust my voice to make other people feel more comfortable? For example: If your boss has poor hearing, find ways to compensate. Avoid locations with background noise, maintain eye contact, talk a bit louder, enunciate more clearly, reposition your chairs . . . do whatever is necessary to make communication more comfortable and more successful.

(13) Do I adapt my voice to suit the listeners' moods? Pay attention to the people you talk with. Adjust your speaking style so it reflects their moods. If they are obviously troubled about something serious, don't annoy them with a humorous tone.

(14) Do I think before I speak? (CAUTION: If you're in the middle of a heated argument, *don't* answer the phone. Wait until you have the chance to get your emotions under control.)

(15) Who has a voice that I really like? What makes that voice so pleasant? Can I develop some of those characteristics?

(16) Who has a particularly annoying voice? Am I able to concentrate on that person's *message*—or do I simply disregard everything that person says? (Unfortunately, some very smart people have annoying vocal habits. Make a conscious effort to concentrate on

their message—otherwise, you might miss some terrific information.)

(17) If someone else spoke the way I speak, would I listen? Even more to the point—would I like it?

Observing your own vocal skills

Once you understand your vocal personality, it's time to take a closer look at your specific vocal skills. Use this checklist to evaluate your own voice. (If you don't trust your ability to judge your own voice, then ask a colleague to help you with this checklist.)

SPEECH ANALYSIS CHECKLIST—MY VOCAL SKILLS

Rate of speech.

_____ just right

_____ too slow

_____ too fast

TIP: Time yourself with a stopwatch. Count the number of words per minute. Most people speak between 120 and 150 words per minute. President John F. Kennedy was a notoriously fast talker—often topping 200 words per minute. You certainly don't want to be that extreme. But, in general, talking a bit fast is better than talking too slow. Why? Speed projects charisma. Slowness projects lethargy, and can frustrate listeners.

Volume.

_____ just right

_____ too soft

_____ too loud

SUGGESTION: You certainly don't want to shout at your listeners. But in general, being a bit loud is better than being too soft—at least people can hear you. However, by strategically using a soft voice, you can compel others to listen even more closely. Remember how White House counsel Charles Ruff opened President Clinton's impeachment defense? He sometimes spoke so quietly that senators had to lean forward to hear him.

Diction.

_____ Don't slur contractions (couldn't, shouldn't, wouldn't).

_____ Don't omit consonant sounds. Pay special attention to words like gifts, acts, adopt, restless. This was often a problem for Geraldine Ferraro when she campaigned for the vice presidency. She would swallow whole sounds—"Lemme tell ya"—and sometimes leave audiences wondering what she had said.

_____ Don't reverse sounds. Say "prescription," not "perscription"; "ask," not "ax"; "remuneration," not "renumeration"; "nuclear," not "nucular"; "perspire," not "prespire."

_____ Don't add sounds ("athlete," not "athalete"; "film," not "fillem"; "across," not "acrost"). . . . "escape," not "excape" . . . "drowned," not "drowneded."

Pitch.

_____ just right

_____ too high

_____ too deep

You need to be aware that people will make all sorts of judgments about you based solely on the tone of your voice.

A high speaking pitch during a job interview can make you sound too immature for the job. On the other hand, an unnaturally low voice can sound unduly serious.

CAUTION: Be especially careful to bring your tone *down* at the end of declarative sentences. If you end a sentence with your voice going *up*—on a "rising inflection"—you will sound tentative and weak, like you are questioning your own statement.

Rhythm.

_____ just right

_____ monotone (This makes a speaker seem both boring and bored—a double whammy!)

_____ singsong (Unless you are a kindergarten teacher, you will want to stay away from this up-and-down rhythm.)

Quality (or what singers call "timber").

_____ just right

_____ breathy (To overcome breathiness, try projecting your voice directly toward your listeners. Aim at the back of the room for more power.)

_____ nasal (Talking through your nose can really annoy listeners. To fix this problem, try opening your mouth wider so you can get the vowel sounds out.)

_____ hoarseness (Don't overuse or abuse your voice. Make it a good habit to periodically rest your voice throughout the day. This becomes especially important at all-day meetings. Pace yourself.)

CAUTION: This is the hardest area of any self-evaluation. You might want to seek professional help in analyzing the quality of your voice. [See Section Eight]

Non-words (or "fillers").

_____ not a problem for me

_____ "uh"

_____ "ah"

_____ "er"

_____ "um"

_____ "I know"

_____ "you know"

_____ "like"

_____ "well"

Talk-show host David Letterman is notorious for "fillers"—sticking in as many as eight or ten a minute. As a comedian, he's turned it into an exaggerated "vocal trademark" of sorts. But, for the average speaker, fillers are liabilities.

TIP: If you are struggling for ways to drop fillers from your speech, try my "dollar technique." Have someone count the number of fillers you use in a meeting or during a phone call—and then send a matching number of dollars to an organization you don't like. Trust me: it won't take long until those fillers disappear.

Regional accents.

_____ not a problem

_____ slight accent

_____ heavy accent

How can you tell if your accent is too heavy? Listeners will look confused, or miss the message, or ask to have statements repeated—all signs of a serious communication problem.

A word of encouragement here: Light regional accents add vocal appeal. They reflect the speaker's heritage and make the message more memorable. Ann Richards, as the state treasurer of Texas, brought life to her keynote address at the Democratic National Convention with this opening: "Buenos noches, mis amigos! I am delighted to be here with you this evening, because after listening to George Bush all these years, I figured you needed to know what a real Texas accent sounds like."

Observing others.

Take a lesson from seasoned trial lawyers. They weren't born great; they learned by studying others. They sat in the back of courtrooms many times to watch the master lawyers—and those observations yielded valuable techniques.

Try the following quiz. The next time you listen to a speaker, see if you spot any of these common problems with the way they talk:

_____ too loud

_____ too soft

_____ flat and boring

_____ singsong

_____ whiny and complaining

_____ tentative

_____ bossy and abrasive

_____ high-pitched and squeaky

_____ artificially low

_____ mumbling

_____ breathy

_____ nasal-sounding

_____ too fast

_____ too slow

How would *you* evaluate their speaking problems?

Look for patterns. Did their voice get worse when they had to present bad news? Did they speak better when they were more confident with the subject material? Did they start out sounding fine—and then get worse because they hadn't rehearsed the end of their presentation? Did their volume drop whenever they had to bend their head down to read their notes? Was their voice strained because an improperly adjusted microphone forced their neck into an awkward position?

Listen to others. Pay attention. And learn from their mistakes.

A few words about laryngitis.

People make jokes about laryngitis. They shouldn't. Laryngitis is a serious situation. If some condition keeps you from speaking comfortably and effectively, then you need to consult a doctor. Do not delay. The longer you wait for treatment, the more your voice can be damaged.

Many factors can hurt your vocal function: a bad cold, seasonal allergies, cheering too much at a football game, overusing your voice in lengthy meetings, affecting an unnatural pitch, smoking cigarettes, clearing your throat excessively, even stress.

I never had laryngitis until a few years ago, when a simple head cold grew into something much worse. First I noticed a tickle in my throat, but I didn't pay it much attention. Then I noticed some hoarseness, but I didn't pay that much attention, either. I kept on talking as though nothing were wrong—which proved to be a serious mistake. It took weeks of vocal rest to undo the damage from just a few days of vocal abuse. I learned my lesson.

I hope you never get laryngitis, but if you do, put these simple guidelines into practice.

- **Contact a doctor immediately.** To save your voice, ask a friend to schedule your appointment. Also, have someone accompany you to the doctor, so you don't have to talk as much at the appointment.
- Doctors typically advise laryngitis sufferers to **refrain from talking**. That's good advice—but easier said than done! Here are some creative ways to give your voice a much-needed rest:
  * Let friends and business associates know you have laryngitis. Don't waste your voice telling them in words, of course. Send them a note. Or simply point to your throat, smile, and remain silent. They'll get the message. If they still try to enlist you in conversation, just stare at them. Eventually they'll leave you alone.
  * Use simple hand signals: thumbs-up, thumbs-down. Throughout his presidency, Bill Clinton suffered many vocal problems. In an effort to save his voice for an upcoming debate, Clinton once resorted to hand signals—a clever way of responding to passersby, while still giving his overused vocal cords a much-needed break.
  * Carry a notepad and write your conversation.
  * Never raise your voice to respond to a question from another room. Use a clapping system to substitute for speech: one clap means "yes," two claps mean "no."
  * Never waste your voice calling to someone across the street. Give a big smile and a big wave—

but don't even think of yelling a single word.

* Find substitutes for phone calls. Rely on e-mail. Send memos or faxes.
* Eat lunch alone. Take a walk instead of talking with coworkers.
* Ask a colleague to speak on your behalf at a meeting.
* Avoid locations with background noise—particularly crowded restaurants. *Don't even try* to talk over music. You don't want to strain to be heard.

- **Avoid smoky rooms.**
- Doctors often advise laryngitis sufferers to **drink lots of water**. The throat specialist I consulted urged me to carry bottled water everywhere—a good habit I maintain to this day. Stay away from iced drinks, because very cold temperatures can cause your throat to tighten. A much better choice: warm tea (non-caffeinated) with honey. (By the way, water is especially critical to vocal health on plane trips, where the air is quite dry).

Some final tips.

Run through these reminders periodically to keep your voice in optimum condition.

- Your grade-school teacher was right. **Posture really is important.** Poor posture will hurt your air supply. Stand up straight. (Talking on the phone? Be sure to sit up straight. No, they can't *see* the difference ... but they'll sure be able to *hear* it.)
- **Look at people when you talk with them.** Stop shuffling papers or fiddling with stuff on your desk. Looking at your listeners accomplishes several things: (1) It

directs sound more efficiently. (2) It provides listeners with facial expressions, which reinforce any message. (3) It's just plain more courteous.

- **Open your mouth wide when you speak.** Need an example to help here? Watch Madonna in *Evita*. She opens her mouth wide and the sound pours out. If you keep your mouth too constricted, you'll hinder the sound and make it harder for people to understand you.)

- **Use a vocal range that feels natural to you.** Don't try to put on an "impressive" voice; your efforts probably won't work. After all, it takes a lot of professional training to extend a vocal range. Besides, if you try to impress people with a contrived voice, your efforts may only backfire—and you'll end up alienating listeners with a voice that sounds pretentious.

- **Breathe normally.** Don't think you have to take a deep breath before speaking. Breathing is natural. If your breathing feels unnatural, you're doing something wrong.

- **Cut the fillers** ("ah," "like," "you know," "um"). Replace them with a bit of silence. There's nothing like a good pause to grab an audience's attention—and recharge a speaker.

- Want to give your message greater impact? **Change the pitch of your voice on the most important words.** This will direct the listeners' attention to your key points.

- Talk too fast? **Use shorter phrases ... and pause more often.** This will let your listeners keep up with your message.

- Does your voice lack authority? Make sure you're not using a "rising pitch" pattern in your sentences.

Remember: *Drop* your voice *down* at the ends of declarative sentences. Otherwise, your statements will sound like tentative questions . . . and your voice will fail to project confidence.

Using Humor

> *"Laughter is the shortest distance between*
> *two people."*
> —Victor Borge

"How you say it" often involves humor. Indeed, a smile often works when nothing else does. I'm not talking about elaborate jokes. In fact, as a general rule, I caution speakers from using jokes. Why? Because it requires a great deal of skill to deliver a joke—and honestly, most of us don't have that skill. Is there anything worse than a speaker who botches the punch line, or the awkward silence that falls where the laughter should have been?

But speakers don't need to rely on formal jokes to get a smile. The following examples show a wide range of options—and give some ideas for creating your own light-hearted touches of humor.

- **Use real-world analogies and visual imagery.**
  * "I'm here to talk about *Insurance Companies in the Fast Lane.*"
  * "No Monday-morning quarterbacks at this meeting, please."
- **Try word play.**
  * Working to overcome the image of stiffness that

marked his 1996 campaign for the Republican presidential nomination, Malcolm Forbes began using humor very effectively in 1999. My favorite example? When Forbes defined estate taxes as "taxation without respiration."

* Bob Dole got a terrific laugh by referring to three ex-presidents (Gerald Ford, Jimmy Carter, and Richard Nixon) as "see-no-evil," "speak-no-evil," and "evil."

* When asked by talk-show host David Letterman how he preferred to be addressed, Vice President Al Gore offered this: "Your Adequacy."

To create your own wordplay, simply take a familiar expression and do a verbal flip-flop:

* "On a scale of 1 to 10, this project got a 'minus-3' rating."

* "Our medical system needs some old-fashioned resuscitation. How can we breathe life back into healthcare reform?"

* "Excuse the pun, but . . . why are teachers getting so testy these days?"

- **Use a natural voice.** Take a first-person approach and get involved. Use "I" liberally. Show a real voice.

- **Involve the audience.** Use the word "you" often.
  * "Unless you're a mind-reader, you will want to ask a lot of questions."
  * "Did you think last year's fund-raiser was good? Wait till you see what's in store for *this* year!"

- **Refer to current events.** It was Will Rogers who once said, "There is no credit to being a comedian, when you have the whole government working for you. All you have to do is report the facts. I don't even have to exaggerate."

When Barbara Bush was asked to give a speech at Wellesley College's graduation ceremonies, she overcame objections to her "first lady" status with this quip: "Somewhere out in this audience may even be someone who will one day follow in my footsteps and preside over the White House as the president's spouse. [Pause] I wish him well."

- **Create dialogue.** The more you can share a conversational style with your audience, the more they will respond.

    * "Employees often say to me, 'Frank, we want to get more involved.' Well, today I can say, 'Here's your chance.'"

- **Use candor.**

    President John F. Kennedy once said, "When we got into office, the thing that surprised me most was to find that things were just as bad as we'd been saying they were."

- **Try a light, self-deprecating touch.** But don't overdo it. If you knock yourself too much, the audience may begin to question your competence or your reputation. A light-hearted touch is perfect.

    * After Adlai Stevenson lost the presidential election for the second time, he said, "I think I missed my calling. As a matter of fact, I think I missed it twice."

    * Sonny Bono marveled at being elected to Congress as a Republican: "The last thing in the world I thought I would be is a U.S. congressman, given all the bobcat vests and Eskimo boots I used to wear."

    * When Secretary of State Madeleine Albright introduced herself to hundreds of staffers during her first week on the job, she gave a mock curtsy and

quipped, "You may notice that I don't exactly look like Secretary [Warren] Christopher."

CAUTION: Good humor brings people together; it doesn't divide. Stay away from sarcastic comments, negative stereotypes, and mean-spirited barbs. Above all, avoid sexist, racist, or ethnic jokes. They will come back to haunt you.

When You Say It

"TIMING: The alpha and omega of aerialists, jugglers, actors, diplomats, publicists, generals, prizefighters, revolutionists, financiers, dictators, lovers."
—Marlene Dietrich, actress

■　　■　　■

Timing Is Everything

There are really only two times to say anything: the right time, and the wrong time. The wrong time falls into two categories—saying something too soon, and saying something too late. If you want to say something, say it at the right time.

* The right message + the right timing = communication power
* The right message + the wrong timing = missed opportunities

You can strengthen any message with strategic timing.

* When New York congresswoman Carolyn Maloney wanted to focus public attention on domestic violence in the military, she maximized her message by delivering it one day after a *60 Minutes* segment on the same topic.

* Vice President Al Gore addressed civil-rights spending on Martin Luther King Jr. Day—speaking from Reverend King's former pulpit, no less.

People who say something at "the right time" make their messages more powerful. Here are some basic questions to help you focus on the best timing for your messages.

(1) Can I adapt my message to suit the time of day?
(2) Can I connect my message to a seasonal theme?
(3) Can I relate my message to a news event?
(4) Can I tie in my message to an anniversary?
(5) Can I capitalize on media coverage to draw attention to my message?
(6) Can I make my message more timely by citing new research?
(7) Would this message have been more effective (or less effective) if I had given it sooner? Why?
(8) Would this message become stronger (or weaker) if I waited until a later date? What would I gain by waiting? What could I lose?
(9) Am I ready to "go public" with my message? (In the words of author Lillian Hellman, "I like people who refuse to speak until they are ready to speak.")

THE TIME OF DAY

What time of day will you be speaking? Will it make a difference? Absolutely. Consider the pitfalls—and prevent problems.

- **breakfast/early morning**
  - * Listeners may be groggy. One speaker went to a high school to discuss environmental issues and became unnerved when some students actually slept during her early-morning presentation.
  - * People may be in a rush. This is not the time for leisurely humor or lengthy details. At breakfast, more than any other time of day, it's wise to heed Franklin Delano Roosevelt's advice: "Be sincere, be brief, be seated."
  - * Listeners may be preoccupied with work demands of the day. Again, this will affect their receptivity. At a job interview, for example, you need to be particularly sensitive to the interviewer's time limitations.
  - * Attendees may be irritable. Why? Because they had to change their morning commute to attend the meeting.
- **mid-morning**
  - * Listeners may need a coffee break. If at all possible, provide coffee and tea. Otherwise, your listeners will simply head to the nearest cafeteria, missing a chunk of your presentation.
  - * Attendees may need to use the restrooms. A safe rule of thumb: If your listeners have been sitting for more than an hour, give them a quick three-minute break before you talk. Otherwise, they'll just leave in the middle anyway—interrupting other folks in the audience and distracting you.
  - * People may need to check in for messages. Again, a three-minute break is a good investment—it gives them a chance to make a quick call without bother-

ing the whole room. But don't give them too long—otherwise they may get bogged down with work details.

- **immediately before lunch**
  * Listeners are hungry and probably can't concentrate well. Don't be surprised if no one asks any questions before lunch. It doesn't mean they're bored. It only means they'd rather go eat. A smart alternative: Invite people to ask questions throughout your presentation—just be prepared to keep the questions in check so you don't run overtime. Audiences will forgive you for almost anything—except making them late for lunch.
  * Listeners have been sitting all morning and may need to stretch. An easy solution? Invite them to stand up and take a thirty-second "stretch break" right at their seats.
  * Listeners may be experiencing "information overload." Supplement your remarks with handouts so people can easily review your material later.
- **during lunch**
  * Lunch presents problems for listeners, who invariably want to eat. Never talk when your listeners are trying to enjoy the main part of their meal. If you must talk during dessert, that's passable—just be prepared for the sounds of clinking forks and rattling coffee cups.
  * Lunch also presents a doublebind for speakers. After all, you need food for energy. But you can't eat a big meal right before you speak because it will just sit there like a big lump. (Plus, there's always the added problem of having food stuck in your teeth. It's hard

to command attention at the lectern when the audience is preoccupied with that big green piece of spinach stuck in your front teeth.) Best option? Consider having a light snack before you arrive—and skip the heavy meal. Use your table time to relax and find out what the other people are thinking.

* Participants want to talk with their friends. Try to make your luncheon talk as informal and conversational as possible—so listeners feel like you're at the table with them.

* Luncheon groups want to have fun. Give them fun—anecdotes, real life examples, clever quotes. Remember: Lunch is supposed to be a relaxing break in their day.

• **immediately after lunch**

* Listeners may be drowsy after eating a big meal. Make the opening of your speech lively—just to grab their attention.

* Post-lunch attendees may not be able to arrive on time. If you don't want your opening to be interrupted, consider starting a few minutes late. When I spoke at the 1999 International Association of Business Communicators conference in Washington, D.C., a standing-room-only crowd prevented latecomers from entering the room. Rather than have my opening disrupted, I chose to start a few minutes late—and used those minutes to personally usher late arrivals into the room.

* Listeners may have a hard time switching from an "entertainment mode" to a "learning mode." Maybe you can open with something lighthearted, so the transition isn't unbearable for them.

- **afternoon**
  - Listeners will need another coffee break. Again, make coffee available—or risk the likelihood that they'll interrupt your message as they head to the nearest deli.
  - People may be overwhelmed with data. Rather than hit them with lots of hard data upfront, consider a low-key opening so they can ease into your message. Also, provide lots of handouts, so they can review the details at a later date.
  - Attendees may need to leave early to start their commute home. Nothing's worse than running overtime at the end of the day. Folks want to head home—let them.

- **early evening**
  - Attendees may arrive late (and tired) from working all day. Respect their situation.
  - Parents with young children may need to go home early to put their children to bed. Have a table at the back of the room so early departures can take any promotional materials without distracting the rest of the audience.

- **after-dinner speech**
  - Audiences may have been drinking alcohol at a cocktail reception. Be prepared for loud chatter.
  - People may simply want to socialize—and may resent a serious speech (particularly one that runs too long).

"In the theater, I've found that, in general, reaction and laughter come easier at an evening performance, when the audience is more inclined to forget its trou-

*bles. Matinee customers must enter the theater in a
more matter-of-fact frame of mind, hanging on tightly
before they let themselves go."*
—BEATRICE LILLY, ENGLISH ACTOR AND COMEDIAN

TIE IN YOUR MESSAGE TO SEASONAL ISSUES

September is an excellent month to introduce anything
related to learning. No matter how old we get, we still associate September with going back to school and learning
new things. December is a great month to solicit donations
for charity—but a bad month to get people to attend
meetings.

Publishers have long known that January is an excellent
month to introduce "how-to" books. Why? Because the holiday rush is over, and folks are in the mood to set better
habits for themselves. Speakers can tap into this January
mind-set to share various "how-to" tips with listeners.

Spring is a smart time to introduce fitness topics. A hospital speakers bureau, for example, might capitalize on
spring by launching programs on weight loss and exercise.

Almost every topic can have a seasonal hook. Capitalize
on that natural interest.

TIE IN YOUR MESSAGE TO ANNIVERSARIES

Prince Philip, Duke of Edinburgh, used the twenty-fifth
anniversary celebration of the World Wide Fund for Nature
to mobilize representatives of the major religions in defense
of the environment.

Israel's fiftieth anniversary proved to be the occasion for
a variety of awards and special events.

TIE IN YOUR MESSAGE TO PUBLIC CELEBRATIONS

President Clinton volunteered to spend Martin Luther King Jr. Day painting classrooms in Washington, D.C. Clinton's reasoning? "We really wanted to emphasize that Martin Luther King's birthday is a day of service—a day on, not a day off."

Earth Day celebrations gave Cardinal John O'Connor of New York effective timing to make an anti-abortion statement: "One of the most dangerous environments in the world today is the mother's womb. Millions of babies are killed there each year."

- **What's the best time of day if I want to avoid public scrutiny?**

Sometimes speakers really don't want anyone to hear their messages. President John F. Kennedy once joked that he waited until "about two in the morning" to announce the selection of his brother, Robert Kennedy, to serve as U.S. attorney general—and then he just wanted to stick his head out the door and whisper, "It's Bobby."

Of course, we laugh at the idea of a two A.M. press conference, but I actually had firsthand experience with a similar situation. Wanting to learn more about a zoning issue, I attended a governmental meeting that began at seven-thirty one January night. In spite of the cold weather, the room was packed with other residents—all of us wanting to express concern about this controversial matter. Alas, we never got the chance. The topic was *last* on the agenda and never came up for public discussion until—yes—close to 11:00 P.M. Need I tell you the room had thinned out by that time?

Teachers tell me this is a favorite practice among some school boards. While parents and teachers might show up in large numbers to monitor controversial educational issues, they often wind up having to leave before their topic is allowed to reach the floor.

- **What's the best day of the year if I want to obscure my message?**

There's no one answer to this question. Evasive folks can find lots of creative ways to obscure messages. Corporations have long chosen to announce bad news on the Friday after Thanksgiving. Why? Because the average person is busy with holiday activities, not reading the fine print in newspapers.

Local government groups can easily escape public attention by holding controversial meetings during the week of July 4—when many constituents are on vacation. One community activist told me that her town routinely chose this prime vacation week for assorted nefarious activities, such as cutting down trees or demolishing historic buildings, thereby evading public scrutiny and escaping negative media coverage.

Indeed, I was once very involved in community efforts to prevent a controversial demolition project. A town meeting was scheduled to discuss the plan on back-to-school night in September. Could there be any worse night for harried parents to attend a meeting? Oh well, I suppose we can be grateful they didn't hold it on New Year's Eve.

My point is this: By controlling the timing, you control the message.

Of course, you might not get the luxury of choosing your own timing—in which case, you'll want to have strong impromptu skills.

Impromptu Speaking

Mark Twain once said, "It takes three weeks to prepare a good ad-lib speech." But my guess is, you won't have three weeks. So, how can you respond—with intelligence and grace—when someone shoves a question at you?

Here are seven useful guidelines:

(1) Feel free to pause for a few seconds to collect your thoughts. There's no law that says you have to speak immediately.

(2) Be decisive. Once you pick your main theme, stick with it. Don't change subjects in midstream.

(3) Open with a general statement. This helps *you* (by giving you extra time to organize your thoughts), and it also helps *your audience* (by giving them a "preview" of your message.)

(4) Offer just two or three points of evidence. Please don't get bogged down in confusing chronological details. Avoid anything that sounds like this:

"Back in May of 2000—or maybe it was June, I can't be sure, it could even have been July, I don't really remember—our community conducted a survey." This is hardly the way to inspire confidence in your listeners!

(5) Look at the whole room—not just at the person who asked the question.

(6) Wrap up your thoughts with a firm conclusion.

(7) Once you've offered your conclusion, don't amend it. Avoid the temptation to add, "Just one more point . . ." *Stop*. Period.

Awkward Timing

Sometimes you don't have the luxury of good timing. Circumstances may be awkward or downright embarrassing, but you still have to proceed.

When President Clinton addressed the opening of the fifty-third session of the United Nations' General Assembly, the whole nation was preoccupied with television coverage of his testimony in the Monica Lewinsky scandal. But the UN delegates gave Clinton a standing ovation—a rare expression for the UN, and a welcome reception for a beleaguered president.

Chances are, the average speaker won't have to suffer the spectacle of televised grand-jury testimony. But you may well find yourself forced to speak at an awkward time. If that's the case, hold your head high . . . don't refer to the mess . . . and try to focus on positive points.

Above all, don't complain or whine. It will work against you.

Frequency

How often do you communicate your message? Or how seldom?

Back in the 1960s, Ronald Reagan began giving speeches against "big government." Folks liked his message. It played well. And from then on, he never let up—seeking every possible opportunity to repeat that key message.

Advertisers have long known that repetition is a key selling point. To sell a product or service, advertisers must *reach* the right audience—and do so *frequently*. The same applies to speeches. To "sell your message," you must *reach* the right audience—and do so *frequently*.

During the heat wave of summer 1999, President Clinton addressed almost five thousand people on the Pine Ridge Reservation in South Dakota. Whatever well-intentioned words Clinton wanted to offer the Native Americans were undercut by a governmental history of infrequent communication.

When You Must Deal with Resistance

If someone resists your message, respect their opinion. Be polite. Listen. Don't lose your temper. Above all, don't give up. A no doesn't have to stay a no. With optimistic persistence, you can turn it into a maybe . . . or even a yes.

Communication isn't a one-shot deal. It's a continuum. People often get discouraged too soon and simply give up. And that's unfortunate, because good communication takes work.

If your first method doesn't succeed, keep looking. Find other ways to sell your message—and over time you will make headway.

When It's Better to Wait

Shirley MacLaine once said, "It's useless to hold a person to anything he says while he's in love, drunk, or running for office." This is true.

It's also useless to expect anyone to listen while he's got

bigger problems on his mind. How can you expect a friend to listen to your complaints the same day he got a big dent in his car? Or the same week his job got slashed? How can you expect your boss to respond positively if you ask a favor the minute she walks in the door from her vacation? Or the day she returns to the office after a death in the family?

Be flexible. Know when to wait.

If someone has said something particularly upsetting to you, don't react right away. Take a "time-out." Find a quick way to escape the situation—perhaps by putting the caller on hold, or excusing yourself from the meeting. Use that "found time" to catch your breath.

Or, as an alternative, simply stay quiet and listen. You may gain the upper hand in a difficult situation just by letting the other person vent. How? By listening, you will gain important insight into what the other person thinks. Knowledge is power.

When You Have to Say "No"

Many of us have a hard time saying no. But from time to time, we all have to say it—and with practice, we can get better at it. We can say no in a way that lets us feel more comfortable . . . and makes other people less upset.

Over the years, I've tried saying no in a variety of ways; some have worked, some have backfired. Here are a few of the techniques that have worked especially well.

• "No, but . . ."
Go from the particular request (which you *can't* do) to a general contribution (which you *can* make). Example: "No,

I really can't organize the school fair. But I'll be very glad to manage one of the booths."

- **"I'd like some time to think about it."**

Remember, you don't have to answer on the spot. By taking some time to consider the request, you defuse the situation—and also gain the option of saying no in writing or by voice mail (which is a whole lot easier than saying no in person).

- **"Thank you for thinking of me. It's just not possible for me to do it now."**

I have recommended this line to family and friends over the years, and they have gotten consistently good results. It's a particularly graceful way to say no. Another variation: "I'm so flattered you thought to ask me. It's just not possible for me to volunteer right now."

- **"I can't, but these folks . . ."**

If *you* can't do it, at least you can recommend *others* who might help in some way. Example: "I'm not the person to run your blood drive this year . . . but I do have good contacts at the newspapers who could give you valuable publicity. I'll be glad to make those calls for you." Then follow through with your promise—and make those calls.

- **"Not now, but I can next year."**

This is a positive way to handle a request (providing you're *sincere* about helping next time).

- **"I am [STATE YOUR PROBLEM] and I need [STATE YOUR PRIORITIES]."**

Be honest and direct about your situation: "I am dealing with a very ill parent right now. I need to focus my energies on handling these family concerns." And then just stop talking. Resist the temptation to keep justifying your position. Your silence will send a loud message.

- **"I only take advice from [NAME YOUR PROFESSIONAL]."**

Bothered by unwanted medical advice? Unsolicited parenting tips? Inappropriate legal suggestions? Nip that conversation in the bud with: "I only take medical advice from professionals" . . . "I only take parenting advice from Dr. Brazelton" . . . "I only take legal advice from my attorney." You can also shoot the offender a withering glare, just for good measure—but that's optional.

- **"Excuse me" (followed by a quick escape).**

This option is so simple that you might overlook it. When some bore is pestering you and you can't think of a graceful way to say, *"I'm not interested, you sound like an idiot,"* simply say "excuse me" in a polite voice and walk away quickly. You'll feel much better, and believe me: he'll get the picture.

When You Have to Say "I'm Sorry"

Perhaps the two most magic words in the English language are "I'm sorry." And yet many people don't seem to have this phrase in their vocabulary. (I'm not naming names here . . . you know who you are.)

Saying "I'm sorry" can:

* clear the air;
* show your genuine concern;
* eliminate bad feelings;
* foster trust;
* encourage honesty;
* allow communication to go forward.

"I'm sorry" can also do a great deal to assuage your own guilty feelings—but that's a topic I'll leave to clergy and counselors. Here's what I'd like to concentrate on: How can you use an apology to improve communications?

I've learned a lot of things about apologies over the years. Some of them I had to learn the hard way—at great personal cost. But I learned them, and I'm glad to share them.

- **When in doubt, apologize.** Saying "I'm sorry" only takes a few seconds and doesn't cost any money. What's to lose? It might make you feel better. And it most assuredly will make the other person feel better. So don't deliberate. Say it.
- **The sooner you say it, the better.** It's better for you, because you'll stop stewing about it. And it's better for the other people because they'll stop stewing about it.
- **Better late than never.** You may think it's too late to apologize. Wrong. It's never too late to apologize. Remember: "I'm sorry" are the two most magic words in the English language. They can work miracles— even months or years after the fact. Indeed, a colleague once told me that a family riff had separated his siblings for decades. Eventually, one of them said "I'm sorry"—and normal family life resumed with surprising ease.
- **Make an apology even if the other person hasn't noticed your mistake.** Maybe you think you can slip something past the other person. You're right. You might be able to hide the problem—but only for a short while. Eventually they'll find out about the mistake. So you might as well fess up now.

- **Don't make excuses.** People don't want to hear excuses like, "But I didn't have the time," or "But nobody ever told me." People want to hear "I'm sorry," and then they want you to move forward.
- **Make things right.** Try to correct your error. Offer a little something extra—a bonus, a refund, a small gift. Make the other person feel "taken care of" . . . not "taken advantage of."
- **Prevent future screw-ups.** Try to figure out what went wrong, and then fix that situation so it doesn't happen again.
- **Don't say it too often.** "I'm sorry" works best if you don't overuse it. With apologies, frequency often *undercuts* impact.

Procrastination

> *"Even if you're on the right track, you'll get run over if you just sit there."*
> —ARTHUR GODFREY

Delaying communication? Force yourself to "say what must be said" with these techniques.

* Give yourself a deadline. Remember: "One of these days" usually becomes "none of these days."
* Live by the "twenty-four hour rule." Rather than stewing over something indefinitely, give yourself twenty-four hours to communicate your message. It may still be hard and you may not say it very well—but at least you'll get it off your chest.

* Pay a fine. Did you promise yourself you'd call a department meeting this morning, or talk with a difficult colleague this afternoon? Do it—or pay a fine. Charge yourself for each delay—and send the money to charity.
* Put a visual reminder where you can't miss it: on the handle of your refrigerator door, or on the remote control for your television. The trick? Put the notice in a place where it's most annoying—so you literally can't open the refrigerator or use the remote without having to displace your reminder.

Above all, don't use procrastination as an excuse to avoid communicating altogether (e.g., "I've neglected that phone call for so long, I might as well just scrap the whole thing"). "Better late than never" may be a cliché, but it's true.

Someone once confessed to me that he put off buying a wedding gift for seven years. He kept thinking, "I'm already so late, I might as well forget it." But he ultimately sent the gift with a nice note—and received a hearty thank-you.

Say what you've got to say. Do what you've got to do. As novelist George Eliot put it, "It is never too late to be what you might have been."

Where You Say It

"Location, location, location."

■   ■   ■

■   ■   ■

Choosing the Best Location

The right location can create greater impact for any message. The wrong location can botch the whole deal. Before you say one word, take a few minutes to think about *where* you should say it.

Years ago, I heard about someone who had suffered the indignity of being fired in an elevator. Yes, you read that correctly: While taking the elevator down to the lobby at the end of a long work week, she bumped into her boss. Apparently, her boss had gotten too busy to fire her during the day . . . so the "You're out of here" conversation took place in the elevator. I don't believe there's ever a good place to be told you're fired—but surely a public elevator has to rank as one of the worst.

Your job, as a communicator, is to look at each message . . . and figure out the best place to say it. Think creatively. You'll find your message takes on a whole new dimension when it's tailored to the right location.

* When John F. Kennedy wanted to address the issue of his Catholicism, he took his speech smack into the heart of America's conservative Bible Belt—making what turned out to be a landmark address to the Greater Houston Ministerial Association in 1960.

The Hometown Advantage

Sports teams often talk about "the hometown advantage." That same "home turf" dynamic can also benefit speakers.

* When Dan Quayle wanted to jump-start his GOP presidential campaign, he chose to address supporters in the gym at his former high school.
* The memorial service for noted author James Michener was held at The George School in Newtown, Pennsylvania, where Michener taught English for several years back in the 1930s.
* Macedonia paid tribute to its most beloved native daughter by putting up a monument on the site where Mother Teresa's house once stood. The simple inscription? "The world is not hungry only for bread, but for love."
* When the U.S. Postal Service released a new stamp featuring Dr. Seuss's Cat in the Hat, they held the ceremony in Dr. Seuss's hometown of Springfield, Massachusetts.
* When South African Archbishop Desmond Tutu wanted to thank American civil-rights leaders for helping to end apartheid in South Africa, he gave his

speech from the Atlanta pulpit where Dr. Martin Luther King Jr. once preached. Tutu made this connection: "We drew enormous courage from your history. You helped us, ten thousand miles away."

Make the Most of Your Location

To prepare for a visit from Pope John Paul II, the city of St. Louis had to transform the huge Trans World Dome into a churchlike atmosphere—clearing an auto show out of the convention center to turn the space into a temporary church serving over one hundred thousand people.

By comparison, your room preparations should seem pretty simple. Consider these factors:

- **temperature of the room**

Keep it cool. Set the temperature about five degrees lower than usual. The cooler air will keep everyone awake—and compensate for the warm bodies that will soon fill the room. (Hotel rooms can be notoriously hot. Be sure to arrive early so you can fix any problems before the audience gets there.)

- **the lectern**

During the Bush-Dukakis debates, much fuss was made over the height of the lectern. Bush wanted it fifty-two inches high; Dukakis wanted it to be fourty-four inches. No matter what height you choose for your lectern, be sure to personalize it. Design a lightweight plaque that you can easily carry to the event—covering the hotel's name on the lectern with the logo of your organization.

- **windows**

Shut window blinds to eliminate glare—and prevent the audience from staring outside while they should be listening to you.

- **room size**

Ideally, you want a room in which there seems to be moderate crowding. I'm not telling you to choose a small room so you can pack 'em in like sardines! But a room that's well filled will make you feel more successful as a speaker—and create an upbeat atmosphere for the audience. What happens if you're assigned a room that's way too big? Get there early and rope off the back half of the room—encouraging attendees to sit closer together down front.

- **seating**

Again, arrive early so you can adjust the seating to suit your own needs. Add extra chairs. Create an aisle. Rearrange awkward tables. Do all this *before* the audience arrives. Once your listeners are seated, they will not be happy if you ask them to move. Indeed, they will not cooperate. I once heard a minister repeatedly ask his congregation to move closer together in the pews so late arrivals could find seats at the ends. The minister's requests were completely ignored. Of the hundreds of people in attendance, not one person budged more than a quarter of an inch—and folks seemed greatly pained at having to move even that much. Asking an audience to move is like asking a pig to sing: You will only waste your breath, and annoy the pig. In the end, the pig still won't sing—and in the end, an audience still won't move.

- **noisy distractions**

Beware of accordion doors. Hotels use these dividers to

separate one huge room into two smaller units (and thereby collect multiple rental fees). Invariably, the people in the adjacent room will be holding a tuba convention—or otherwise distracting your audience with noise at 130 decibels. So, get friendly with the hotel's management beforehand and insist on a quiet space.

• **doors**

Shut all doors before you begin to speak. Why compete with hallway noise? Even better, station a colleague outside each door to prevent noisy interruptions from latecomers.

If your room still winds up being less than perfect, don't fret about it. I was once asked to speak in a movie theater. I'm not kidding. A real movie theater—complete with horrendous lighting, unmovable seating, non-adjustable heat control, pitiful acoustics, and the overwhelming smell of popcorn. There wasn't a single thing I could do to improve that room, so I just did the best I could under the circumstances and tried to give the audience a good time. It worked.

Bad Locations

The National Rifle Association had long planned to hold a major convention in Denver, Colorado, during April of 1999. Nothing too noteworthy about the location—until a shooting rampage at Columbine High School in nearby Littleton brought renewed attention to the whole issue of gun control. To his credit, Denver mayor Wellington Webb persuaded the NRA to downsize its convention.

Technical Glitches

President Clinton stood up to make a major address on health care—only to discover that the TelePrompTer had the wrong speech. Until George Stephanopoulos could fix the mess (about seven minutes later), President Clinton had to fly on his own.

Now, you will probably never use a TelePrompTer—but don't feel complacent about technical glitches. They're out there—just waiting to catch you:

- **sound**
  * When the sound went off in their first 1976 debate, President Ford and challenger Jimmy Carter stood there like statues for almost half an hour—waiting for the glitch to be fixed.
  * Hotel conference rooms around the country were packed with pro-choice advocates, all waiting to hear Representative Pat Schroeder on giant TV screens. Unfortunately, a technical glitch caused the sound to fail at all fourteen locations, and audiences couldn't hear a word.
  * At the 1996 Republican National Convention in New Orleans, a failing audio system left the audience watching—but not listening.
- **lighting**
  * The Minnesota Orchestra began their performance at Carnegie Hall—only to watch the stage slide into darkness. What happened? Someone backstage had bumped into the lightboard, and it took a while until the computerized lighting system could be reset.

- **props**
  * When Bucks County (PA) commissioner Sandra Miller and her running mate, Christopher Serpico, announced their candidacy, they festooned the county courthouse with red, white, and blue balloons—only to be surprised when the balloons drifted upward and set off fire alarms, forcing an evacuation of the building.
- **stage mishaps**
  * Bob Dole's race for the presidency was not enhanced by a speech where he leaned against a loose railing and tumbled off the stage.
  * President Gerald Ford's reputation for clumsiness motivated his assistants to have Ford's water glass securely fastened at the podium with a brace. (Just to show that you can't prevent every mishap: Ford did not spill any water. However, he did manage to blurt out that Eastern Europe was not dominated by the Soviet Union—an observation that cost him some credibility.)
- **personal items**
  * Kurt Masur, musical director of the New York Philharmonic, had to step away from the stage a moment before the orchestra could play. The low-tech glitch he ran into? He simply forgot his glasses.
- **microphone**
  * Busy prepping for his regular radio broadcast one Saturday, President Reagan made a joke about bombing the Soviet Union—never realizing that his pre-speech comments were being recorded.
  * President Bush had a similar problem with some post-speech comments. Bush complained that the

Q&A session had not gone the way he had expected. An open microphone (accidentally left on) broadcast his whiny comments to eager ears.

- **seating**
    * The New Jersey inaugural for Governor Jim Florio hit a glitch when the carefully planned seating chart was eaten up in the computer—forcing seats to be taken on a first-come, first-served basis. A mad rush ensued—with equally mad partygoers.

Regarding technical glitches, I can only offer this advice: Imagine a worst-case scenario. And plan for it. As Ralph Waldo Emerson observed: "Only shallow men believe in luck."

Speaking Outdoors

Outdoor events can be very appealing, but they take tremendous planning. Here's a basic list to consider.

- **indoor alternatives**—After all . . . what happens if the weather turns stormy?
- **enough seating**—Test the chairs. What are the sight-lines? If folks can't see the speaker, they're less likely to listen.
- **getting the audience's attention**—Consider playing music as the crowd gathers, and then stop it abruptly before the speech. When the crowd hears the music stop, they'll likely stop talking to see what's going on.
- **sound amplification**—Be aware: Voices don't carry

well when you're outdoors. You'll probably need microphones.

- **background noises**—Will your event be near a busy highway, or close to a noisy playground? Careful attention to timing might spare you some frustration.
- **parking**—Will the parking process disrupt your event in any way? Prevent headaches. Pay attention to the details.
- **concession stands**—It's hard to compete with food vendors. You might want to offer longer breaks, so folks can grab their snacks without interrupting the proceedings.

Of course, you can prepare carefully and still run into frustrations. Speaking outdoors is never easy. But if you concentrate on the right message, you'll do fine.

When Pope John Paul II spoke in Mexico, his listeners perched on tree branches, stood on loudspeaker stands, and climbed onto friends' shoulders . . . in short, they did anything necessary to hear the Pope speak. They listened for the message and didn't complain about the lack of comfortable seating—a reassuring triumph of content over comfort.

Out-of-Town Problems

Traveling to out-of-town speaking engagements is both time-consuming and expensive. Too many speakers accept an invitation months in advance . . . and then regret their hasty decision as the date approaches.

Before you agree to travel to any speaking engagement, ask yourself the following questions.

"DO I HAVE TO GO?"

Practical questions for speakers.

(1) What is the total travel time? Be realistic. Travel seldom goes as smoothly as it looks on an airline timetable. Consider all the factors.

(2) How much will the trip cost?

(3) Do I need any assistants for this presentation? . . . audiovisual support? . . . TelePrompTer operators? . . . people to distribute promotional materials? How much will *their* travel cost?

(4) Does the audience justify this expense? Again, be brutally honest here. Not all audiences are created equal. Some will give you greater contacts.

(5) Will I gain valuable press attention by speaking at this event?

(6) Can I combine this trip with any other business? For example: Can I meet with major clients in that city? . . . recruit at a nearby college? . . . attend a sales convention? . . . visit with distributors?

(7) Are there smart alternatives?

When Lawrence Weinbach, the CEO of Unisys Corporation, was honored with the Communicators Award by the International Association of Business Communicators, he was working overseas and could not attend IABC's conference in Washington, D.C. His solution? Videoconferencing. Weinbach's personable presentation style wowed the crowd from halfway around the world.

Attorney Alan Mittelman, from the Philadelphia firm of Spector, Gadon and Rosen, P. C., was a featured speaker at a continuing-education program offered by the Society of Financial Planning Professionals. The format: a national telephone conference call, combined with a slide presentation over the Internet. (A WORD OF CAUTION ABOUT INTERNET PRESENTATIONS: Be careful to protect your intellectual property. "Downloaded" information can quickly lead to "misused" information—where your authorship is lost along the way. Protect yourself. *Copyright* your materials.)

(8) Would a local colleague welcome the chance to substitute for me?

(9) The ultimate test: If I stayed home and didn't give this speech, what would I lose?

Who Says It, and Who Is Listening?

"The public is like a piano. You have to know what keys to poke."

—Al Capp, American cartoonist

■ ■ ■

■　　■　　■

The Right Speaker for the Right Message

Who's talking? And who's listening?

No message exists in a vacuum. It's tied in to the person-ality and image of the speaker. It's also tied in to the needs and expectations of the audience. When the right speaker gives the right message to the right audience, the combina-tion can't be beat.

Who Says It?

When a memorial was created to honor the thirty thousand Londoners killed during World War Two bombings (the Blitz), it was the Queen Mother who unveiled the stone at a special ceremony. Her husband King George VI had reigned throughout the war.

When officials broke ground for a new neuroscience lab at Rutgers University in New Jersey, actor Christopher

Reeve used his personal experience to make the message more compelling. Paralyzed from a horseback-riding accident, Reeve offered this bit of optimism: "In the few years I've been injured, instead of hearing what we are going to do, I'm hearing of patents, FDA trials, how to humanize antibodies . . . and that dialogue is very satisfying to hear. I'm so grateful we have a worldwide effort going on."

Actor Gregory Peck is best known for his film role as the Southern lawyer who fought against racism in the film version of *To Kill a Mockingbird*. Years later, when he was honored with the Marian Anderson Award for his humanitarian efforts, Peck leveraged his position to speak out about gun control: "What is wrong with keeping guns out of the hands of the wrong people?"

The Juvenile Diabetes Foundation received special attention when Miss America 1999 (Nicole Johnson) discussed the illness because she has the same condition.

The Kentucky Derby Festival dedicated their Pegasus Parade to all the troops who served in the Persian Gulf—and got General H. Norman Schwarzkopf to lead as grand marshal.

At the dedication of a new cancer institute at the Good Samaritan Medical Center in West Palm Beach, Florida, actor Robert Urich proved an effective spokesperson. Reflecting on his own efforts to battle cancer, Urich was in a unique position to offer these words of hope: "Cancer is a survivable disease. It cannot destroy hope. It cannot destroy love."

Mothers Against Drunk Driving (MADD) offers "Victim Impact Panels." This well-received program gives victims of drunk driving the chance to share their stories with DUI

(Driving Under Intoxication) offenders. Because the panelists speak from their own tragic experiences, their messages make a greater impact.

SELF-ANALYSIS

Who are you? Do *your listeners* know who you are? Even more important, do they *like* you?

Here is a simple quiz that will help you understand how you come across to others. Be honest with yourself. After all, you can't hide from the folks who listen to you . . . so there's not much point in trying to hide from yourself.

"HOW DO I APPEAR TO AUDIENCES?"

A self-analysis.

(1) I talk about topics that interest other people.

    (very little)   1   2   3   (very much)

(2) I support my points with appropriate facts and examples.

    (very little)   1   2   3   (very much)

(3) I pay close attention to my listeners' reactions and adjust my material accordingly.

    (very little)   1   2   3   (very much)

(4) I accommodate others' needs—allowing for coffee breaks or wrapping up early, if necessary.

    (very little)   1   2   3   (very much)

(5) I make a conscious effort to interact with my audience—asking questions, requesting a show of hands, et cetera.

    (very little)   1   2   3   (very much)

(6) I smile appropriately and make good eye contact.
   (very little)   1   2   3   (very much)

(7) I welcome questions—and don't sound defensive when I answer.
   (very little)   1   2   3   (very much)

(8) I listen actively to their concerns—taking notes and offering to follow up with more information if they want it.
   (very little)   1   2   3   (very much)

(9) I take responsibility for letting my listeners know what action must be taken.
   (very little)   1   2   3   (very much)

(10) I try to motivate my listeners and build consensus.
   (very little)   1   2   3   (very much)

Who Is Listening?

"Your audience gives you everything you need. They tell you. There is no director who can direct you like an audience."
—FANNY BRICE, ACTRESS

MEETING THE AUDIENCE'S NEEDS

Picture this situation: You have only one orange, but two people want it. What's the best way to meet their needs? Well, you could automatically cut the orange into two equal halves. But don't do it yet. Before you do anything, ask *why* they want the orange. Suppose Person Number 1 says, "I'm thirsty," and Person Number 2 says, "I want the skin to bake a cake." In that case, cutting an orange in half wouldn't do much good—but if you give one person the juice and the other person the rind, you will satisfy both people.

As a communicator, you're in a similar situation. Find out *who* you're talking to . . . and *why* they want to hear from you. Don't make assumptions about what they need: Ask. When you understand your listeners, you will communicate more successfully.

AUDIENCE ANALYSIS

Here are seventeen basic questions to ask about an audience.

(1) Have any colleagues talked with this group before?

Ask for their impressions. Gather past speeches. Maybe you'll want to reference some of them.

(2) What's the size of your audience?

The number of attendees won't affect your topic, but it will affect the way you approach your topic. Why? Because small audiences and large audiences have different listening personalities.

In general, the larger the audience, the greater your need to grab their attention with humorous anecdotes, real-life examples and clever "sound bites." Remember: That woman in the thirty-seventh row of a huge auditorium knows you can't see her very well—and if you don't meet her needs, she will simply leave. If she's sitting on an aisle seat, she'll leave physically. If she's stuck in the middle of a row, she'll leave mentally—tuning you out as she fiddles with paperwork or chats with another person or maybe even takes a catnap. Either way, you'll lose the chance to get your message across.

(3) What's the age range?

Choose material that's appropriate to the age group of your audience. For example: Suppose you want to use humor. Should you use a funny line from Will Rogers—or is your audience so young that they never even heard of Will Rogers? Maybe you're talking with retirees. Try to quote experts they can relate to—perhaps an expert source from the American Association of Retired People (AARP).

When President Clinton addressed college students about the need to shore up Social Security and Medicare, he emphasized that they wouldn't be young forever. And he warned that they might get stuck supporting their aging parents at the same time they hoped to raise their own families.

(4) What is the gender mix?

I once heard a male physician discuss the topic of female health issues—citing only male experts. Believe me: Even if he didn't notice this exclusion, his mostly female audience did.

(5) What is the ethnic/religious mix?

When Pope John Paul II made his historic visit to Israel in 2000, he said "It is with profound emotion that I set foot in the land where God chose to pitch his tent." Later, he ended his remarks with "Shalom," the traditional Hebrew greeting.

When talk-show host Oprah Winfrey gave a commencement address at the historically black Morehouse College, she urged the graduates to tap into their spiritual roots: "Real success comes when you learn to act as if everything depends on you, and pray as if everything depends on God."

(6) Will the audience have any special members?

Any high-ranking government officials in attendance? Local celebrities? Spouses? You might want to extend a special welcome.

(7) Will anyone be noticeably absent?

None of the Supreme Court justices attended President Clinton's final State of the Union Address in January 2000. (I'll leave it to President Clinton to speculate on their absence.)

The rest of us need to consider our own audiences. Will key executives be out of town? Will a prominent person be absent because of illness? Could the event be marked by boycotts or protests? You'll want to know about this.

A top executive might be absent because of a business trip. If so, ask the executive to send a delegate as a replacement. You won't get closure on key issues unless the decision makers are represented.

(8) What is the educational background of your audience?

College degrees? Postgraduate work? Or only high-school diplomas? Match your examples to their educational background.

Geraldine Ferraro played to the background of her audience when she spotted a sign from the International Ladies Garment Workers Union in the audience. Ferraro gave a big smile and told them, "Not bad for a garment worker's daughter from Queens!"

(9) What is their professional expertise?

Where do these people work? What are their titles? Are their jobs secure? What career paths do they want to follow? Recognize the unique demands of their jobs. Nothing

alienates listeners more than pontificating about yourself—
while ignoring *their* business problems.

(10) Where do they stand on political issues?

You might not want to raise any political issues, but you
certainly need to be aware of the political orientation in
your audience. And if they take a stand on any legislative
issues, it's imperative that you understand these issues.

(11) How much does your audience already know about your subject?

Even more important: Where did they get this information? Who were their sources?

(12) What has their community accomplished?

What makes these people proud? Does their town boast
a restored theater . . . a new playground . . . a winning football team? Tap in to their community pride.

(13) How often does this group meet?

Every week? If so, they probably know each other pretty
well, and their group dynamics are probably well estab-
lished.

Just once a year? Then maybe they would rather socialize
with seldom-seen friends than listen to a long presentation.

(14) Who spoke at their last meeting?

Get the full agenda of their most recent program. If they
meet often, get several recent agendas. You need to know
who has been influencing them. (Or, at the very least, you
need to know who has been boring them to death.)

(15) Who is scheduled to speak at future meetings?

Find out who's talking at next month's meeting. If it's a
competitor, you want to lay a strong foundation so your
message won't be dismissed by your opponent.

(16) What topics has your audience found most interesting? . . . least interesting?

Don't be shy. Call up the person who invited you and say, "What's been your most interesting topic this year?" And then push a little more: "Tell me the truth. What was your most boring topic?" (CAUTION: Program directors are generally reluctant to acknowledge "boring" speakers, so you can't assume they will volunteer this information. *Ask.*)

(17) Does this group face any special problems?

Have the past three presidents quit under duress? Is membership declining? Have meetings gotten too expensive? Are competitors moving into their turf?

Things are seldom hunky-dory. Dig a little bit. Show you understand their concerns.

AUDIENCE PROFILE SHEET

Full name of group _____

Anticipated size _____ Age range _____

Educational background _____

_____

Professional situation _____

_____

Political orientation/legislative issues _____

_____

Community issues _____

_____

How often does this group meet? _____

_____

Previous speakers/topics _____

_____

Upcoming speakers/topics _____

_____

What topic has this audience found most interesting? Why?

_____

_____

. . . least interesting? Why? _____

_____

Do they have any special problems? _____

_____

What information would be most helpful for them? _____

_____

MAKE "YOU"-ORIENTED STATEMENTS

If you want to connect with your listeners, don't talk so much about yourself. Find ways to address others' needs. TIP: Involve your listeners by using more "you"-oriented lines. Here are some examples.

* "You know from your own experience that _____."
* "You can win by _____."
* "You deserve _____."
* "You'll gain direct access to _____."
* "You can count on _____."
* "You'll be relieved to learn _____."
* "You can take advantage of _____."
* "You can now do something about _____."
* "You can benefit if you _____."
* "You are certainly welcome to_____."
* "You can rely on my department for _____."
* "You can depend on this product to _____."
* "You'll get good value from _____."
* "You know the problem all too well: _____."
* "You've certainly seen for yourselves that _____."
* "You know what will happen if_____."
* "You understand the price we'll pay if_____."
* "You will finally get what you want when _____."

GETTING THE AUDIENCE INVOLVED

Want to get people to stand up and make a commitment? Borrow a trick from old-time evangelist Billy Sunday, who would urge people to "stand up" if they wanted to donate money—and then break into a stirring rendition of the

National Anthem. As soon as folks heard "The Star-Spangled Banner," they would stand up, have a good laugh, and then make a donation.

At a memorial service for John F. Kennedy Jr., attendees were reminded how young John-John had saluted his father's casket many years earlier—and then they were invited to stand and give him their own salute.

At the historic signing of the Middle East Peace Pact, Yitzhak Rabin said: "In the Jewish tradition, it is customary to conclude our prayers with the word 'Amen.' With your permission, men of peace, I shall conclude with the words taken from the prayer recited by Jews daily, and whoever of you who volunteer, I would ask the entire audience to join me in saying 'Amen.'"

Your situations are probably not so dramatic. Nonetheless, you need to involve your listeners. Try these simple ideas.

* Ask them to raise their hands.
* Invite them to write questions on provided notepads.
* Hold a raffle so you can collect their business cards.
* Ask them to introduce themselves to the folks seated nearby.
* Suggest they swap business cards with people at their table.
* Lead them in a corporate cheer.
* Ask them to work in pairs.

Interpreting the Agenda

If you want to grab your listeners' attention, you must understand the spot you occupy in their overall agenda. Be sure to review the material in Section Three, "When You Say it." For your convenience, on the following page is a form that will help you understand quickly your position in the day's agenda.

THE AGENDA

Date of speech _____ Location_____

Suggested time slot_____ Pros/cons _____

_____

Alternate time slots_____ Pros/cons _____

_____

Other presenters/their topics _____

_____

_____

How long are the other presentations? _____

_____

Who/what will precede the speech? _____

_____

Who/what will follow the speech? _____

_____

* IMPORTANT: REQUEST PROGRAM AGENDA, ATTACH A COPY.

Q&A session _____ Moderator _____

Name/phone/e-mail of person who will introduce you _____

_____

* IMPORTANT: TAKE AN EXTRA COPY OF YOUR INTRODUCTION.

On-site rehearsals _____

Meals _____ Coffeebreaks _____Receptions _____

Any time for networking?_____

Any place to distribute promotional literature? _____

TEN THINGS YOU'LL NEVER HEAR FROM ANY AUDIENCE

(1) "We don't need any facts. We'll believe anything you say."

(2) "Go ahead and wing it. We don't mind if you're unprepared."

(3) "Yes, we like dry, boring statistics."

(4) "No, we don't have anything else to do this morning. Feel free to talk as long as you want."

(5) "It doesn't matter which speaker shows up. Our group will be satisfied with any warm body."

(6) "Canned speeches are okay. You don't have to personalize anything for us."

(7) "No, we didn't want to ask any questions anyway."

(8) "Sure—you can use the same old material you've been using for the past couple of years."

(9) "Don't bother doing any homework on our industry."

(10) "It's okay if you bore us to death. Really."

Who Else Could Say It for You?

"It's absurd to divide people into good and bad. People are either charming or tedious."

—Oscar Wilde

■ ■ ■

■　　■　　■

Substitute Speakers

Suppose you come down with a case of the flu . . . or face a family emergency . . . or need a last-minute business trip. Who should fill in for you?

Don't dump this unpleasant responsibility on the program chair. You were invited. You accepted. You canceled. Now you must offer to recommend a substitute. Yes, the organization might prefer to choose their own speaker. But you'll show good manners if you at least *offer* to find a substitute.

Here are some questions that will help you identify alternative speakers.

- **Will anyone want the job?** Don't laugh. If you need to cancel at the last minute, you probably won't have the luxury of choosing from a large pool of talented volunteers. Think of someone who might see this speaking platform as a chance to make business connections, or a chance to get professional recognition.

- **Who has good platform skills?** Ideally, you want a good presenter—someone who the audience will really like. But realistically, the later you cancel, the lower your standards will drop. At the last minute, you might be grateful just to get a warm body at the lectern.
- **Who would the audience respect?** As a general rule of thumb, get the highest-ranking person you can find. Audiences will be less upset by your cancellation if you give them a credible, influential substitute. When illness kept Luciano Pavarotti from appearing at the Grammy Awards, Aretha Franklin filled in and got a standing ovation—one star filling in for another.
- **Who owes you a favor?** Now is the time to cash in your chips.
- **Who can you trust?** A good speaking engagement generates business opportunities. Make sure your substitute will share those leads with you. You don't want to choose a speaker who will undercut your basic message—or steal prospective business.

What Happens if You're Delayed?

When Senator Ted Kennedy was late for a speech to the American Federation of Teachers, who else but President Clinton happened to be in the same hotel giving a speech of his own? Clinton stepped in to serve as pinch-hitter.

Of course, being on time is a cardinal rule for all speakers. But occasionally, emergencies create unavoidable problems.

I pride myself on arriving early for my speeches, but one time I faced a serious delay. Scheduled to speak in Philadelphia at the United Way the morning after Hurricane Floyd ripped up the East Coast, I found that my own timetable was no match for the region's flooded streets and downed wires. I used my cell phone to give the waiting audience "travel reports"—and Christine Brown, president of the United Way of Southeastern Pennsylvania, was kind enough to take over the lectern until I arrived. (Thank you, Christine!)

The lesson? Keep in touch with the program chair so the audience isn't left hanging. And make yourself available afterward, so the audience feels you've been generous with your time.

A Word of Caution about Canceling

President Teddy Roosevelt was shot in the chest in an assassination attempt—and was still determined to follow through with the speech he was scheduled to make. Remarkably, he didn't allow himself to be taken to the hospital until an hour later.

No one says you have to be this stalwart. Nonetheless, when audiences are looking forward to hearing you, they really don't like a cancellation. They expect you to be there. If you can't come, they expect a really good excuse.

Two contrasting examples:

* Elizabeth Taylor cancelled an appearance at an AIDS fund-raiser in France because she couldn't travel after recovering from brain surgery. Taylor issued a statement saying that actress Demi Moore would fill in for her—and the event proceeded.

* Amid publicity that she would quit her job to concentrate on conceiving a baby, newscaster Connie Chung canceled a convention speech. She sent a videotaped apology—only to have it hissed.

Brain surgery is a legitimate excuse; ovulation, apparently, is not.

Choosing the Right Person to Introduce You

Someone is going to introduce you . . . you might as well make sure it's the "right" someone. Please don't leave this to chance. It's extremely important for you to get a good introduction—and you want that intro to come from someone who is well respected and well liked. After all, the audience will judge you partly by the caliber of the person who makes your introduction.

Don't wait until the program chair assigns someone to introduce you. What if you got stuck with the wrong person? Instead, as soon as you accept a speaking engagement, start thinking about who you want to introduce you . . . and ask that person directly. Ask early to prevent scheduling problems.

Always write out your own intro and, again, give it directly to the person introducing you. (You can get a lot of tips on writing an introduction from my earlier book, *Can You Say A Few Words?* [St. Martin's Press].)

Remember: A good introduction will position you the way you want to be seen, and it will reinforce your message. So, by the time you reach the lectern, the audience will already know something positive about you and your message. Think of the person who introduces you as a valued ally—"someone else" who can help you say what you want to say.

Working with Other Speakers

Sometimes you might want additional speakers to support your key messages. Perhaps you could arrange to appear with a panel of experts . . . or you could team up with a colleague to give tandem presentations . . . or you could simply ask a prominent person to share the stage with you.

* When New Jersey governor Christine Whitman announced a budget that supported new initiatives, she invited former governor Thomas Kean to share the platform at her press conference.
* In honor of the Martin Luther King Jr. holiday, his widow, Coretta Scott King, was joined by a prestigious panel in Atlanta: Desmond Tutu of South Africa, former U.S. ambassador Andrew Young, and Nobel Peace Prize–winner John Hume of Northern Ireland.

PANELS

At times, you may be able to choose the panelists who will appear with you. Consider yourself lucky on those rare occasions. You can ask your most talented colleagues to address different aspects of your topic, or invite experts who can lend critical support during the Q&A.

But most times, you will simply be requested to appear—and you will have no say in *who* the other panelists are, or *what* they will talk about.

Whether you get to choose the panelists or simply accept a slot, you need to prepare carefully. Here are some tips to help you succeed:

- Ask to speak first. This allows you to set the tone for the panel—and assures you of adequate time. Yes, I am aware that some panelists prefer to speak last so they can have "the final word." If that's your choice, I'm not going to argue the point. But with over fifteen years of coaching experience, I'll offer this: Few moderators know how to run a good panel. If your panel runs out of time (as often happens with inexperienced moderators), the last speaker will get squeezed. (Forget the middle slots, where your message will likely be lost in the blur.)

- Find out beforehand how the moderator plans to deal with long-winded speakers. Ask if the moderator has a "1 minute" warning card. If not, kindly offer to bring yours. (That's right. Use a 3×5 index card, mark 1 MINUTE in bold letters, and take it to the panel presentation. If the moderator isn't savvy enough to control the time frame, your card will come in very handy.)

- Several weeks prior to the panel, provide the moderator with a fully written introduction. It's important to be introduced the way you want—and the only way to get this kind of an intro is to write it yourself. (Again, you can find a detailed chapter on "Introducing Speakers" in my earlier book, *Can You Say A Few Words?* [St. Martin's Press].)

- Make sure the moderator knows how to pronounce your name. Don't assume. *Make sure.*
- If the moderator didn't cite your credentials adequately, open by adding some brief biographical details. Emphasize the credentials that apply to your role on this panel. Highlight qualifications that will have merit with this audience.
- If another panelist is running overtime, kindly slide the "1 minute" warning card to the moderator. (Now, aren't you glad you prepared for this problem ahead of time?)
- If you're the last speaker and time is running out, just give a brief version of your presentation. Don't try forcing your long version into a short time frame. You'll only frustrate yourself—and annoy your listeners.

Was Your Speech a Success?

"I do not know anyone who has got to the top without hard work. That is the recipe. It will not always get you to the top, but it should get you pretty near."

—Margaret Thatcher, former British prime minister

■　　■　　■

■　　■　　■

"I Could Have Been a Better Communicator if Only . . ."

If I promised you a "magic" technique that would dramatically improve your communication skills in just thirty seconds (and cost you absolutely no money), would you be interested?

Well, here it is. After each presentation (or after each job interview, each sales call, each phone conference . . . whatever), simply complete the following sentence:

> "I could have been a better communicator if only_____
>
> _____
> _____
> _____."

You don't have to tell anyone. You don't even have to write it down every time. But you do have to be honest with yourself—and you do have to answer *right away*. If you wait too long, you will forget all the "little things" that hurt your overall communication.

My recommendation: Periodically write down your responses ... and keep these valuable insights in a special folder. Then, whenever you have to prep yourself for a presentation (or a big meeting or an important sales call), you can quickly review the areas that need special attention—and learn from past mistakes.

Identify Your Speaking Personality

Here are some positive qualities for communicators. On a scale of 1 to 10 (with 10 being the highest score), how would you rate yourself as a communicator?

_____ friendly

_____ credible

_____ knowledgeable

_____ well-prepared

_____ organized

_____ logical

_____ creative

_____ direct

_____ honest

_____ diplomatic

_____ sincere

_____ enthusiastic

_____ respectful

_____ open to new ideas

Assess Your Speaking Style

What makes you successful as a presenter? Learn to capitalize on the strengths of your unique speaking style. Check the description that applies to you.

(1) I am most successful speaking
   _____ one-on-one.
   _____ with small groups.
   _____ to large audiences.

(2) I am most comfortable talking with
   _____ people I know.
   _____ people I don't know.

(3) I prefer speaking engagements where I can
   _____ talk informally.
   _____ speak formally.

(4) I am more successful
   _____ using simple notes.
   _____ working from a detailed outline.
   _____ using a full manuscript.

(5) I would rather audiences think I'm
   _____ well-organized.
   _____ creative.

(6) I tend to value
   _____ feelings more than logic.
   _____ logic more than feelings.

(7) I do better in a Q&A session that has

_____ a lot of pressure.

_____ little pressure.

(8) At a conference with many other speakers, I prefer to

_____ present like everyone else.

_____ do it my own way.

(9) I tend to

_____ show my personal feelings.

_____ keep my private feelings to myself.

(10) I'm more likely to come across as

_____ distant.

_____ accessible.

(11) It's more important that listeners think I have

_____ a grasp of the day-to-day details.

_____ a strategic vision.

(12) It's more important that my listeners think I'm

_____ intelligent.

_____ caring.

(13) My messages are more likely to include

_____ praise.

_____ criticism.

(14) I want my messages to have

_____ an entertainment factor.

_____ a lecture approach.

(15) I usually tend to address an audience's

_____ rights.

_____ responsibilities.

What Are You Doing to Become a Better Speaker?

Good speakers keep getting better by learning from others, taking some risks, and welcoming new ideas for improvement. In short, good speakers keep learning.

Ask yourself: "When is the last time I . . ."

_____ ". . . took a course in public speaking?"

_____ ". . . read a book about presentation skills?"

_____ ". . . spent fifteen minutes analyzing the strengths and weaknesses of another speaker?"

_____ ". . . listened to a really great preacher?"

_____ ". . . watched a videotape of a terrific political speech?"

_____ ". . . spent an hour thinking about audiences I would like to reach?"

_____ ". . . bought books containing lively quotations and humorous anecdotes?"

_____ ". . . had a wardrobe professional choose an excellent presentation outfit for me?"

_____ ". . . saw a top stylist for a hair makeover?"

_____ ". . . allowed myself to experiment with a new presentation technique?"

_____ ". . . had the courage to give a presentation that was different from everyone else's?"

_____ "... assumed a position of leadership in my professional organization so I could develop stronger
speaking skills?"

_____ "... consciously fixed one negative element of my
presentation style?"

_____ "... consulted with a professional about my voice?"

_____ "... asked to be videotaped so I could study my
own body language?"

_____ "... sought help in preparing for Q&A sessions?"

Manage Negative Emotions

Do you let negative thoughts about communicating run
through your mind?

Negative "self-talk" is self-defeating. If you catch yourself thinking of any of the following negative statements,
then it's time to take better control of your communication
skills: "When I think about speaking in public, I feel ..."

_____ "inadequate." ("I just don't have good presentation skills.")

_____ "embarrassed." ("I'm sure I'll look foolish when I
stand up there.")

_____ "fearful." ("I'm most afraid of_____.")

_____ "alone." ("I'm the only one in my department who
can't speak up with confidence.")

_____ "frustrated." ("I know there has to be a better way to
prepare a talk, but I've never had any training.")

_____ "discouraged." ("I've been ashamed of my speaking skills for so long, I don't think I can ever get
better.")

_____ "...insecure." ("If my boss sees how bad I am, this could really hurt my performance appraisal.")

Identify Your Own Strengths

Use this handy checklist to evaluate the specific components of your own speeches, and those you observe.

PERFORMANCE CRITIQUE

Audience _____

Date _____

City _____

Title of Presentation

_____ interesting

_____ mentioned in the introduction

_____ printed on the agenda

Opening

_____ grabs attention right away

_____ targeted to specific audience

_____ projects speaker's confidence

_____ gives a "bottom line" statement upfront

_____ creates a sense of value/urgency/importance

_____ shows originality

Main body

_____ well-organized, easy to follow

_____ uses smooth transitions

_____ makes strong points

_____ well-researched
_____ persuasive, credible
_____ shows fresh perspective
_____ offers distinctive point of view

Conclusion
_____ refers to opening
_____ restates purpose
_____ summarizes main points
_____ asks for audience involvement
_____ makes definite closing statement
_____ makes emotional appeal

Language
_____ short words
_____ plain English
_____ no bureaucratese, no legalese
_____ easy-to-understand sentences
_____ strong verbs
_____ vivid descriptions

Research
_____ good variety of sources
_____ appropriate experts
_____ interesting statistics
_____ real-life examples
_____ anecdotes
_____ quotations
_____ current events, news stories
_____ clever definitions
_____ easy-to-understand comparisons
_____ proverbs

_____ references to pop culture

_____ industry perspective

_____ surveys

_____ endorsements

_____ other research: _____

Humor

_____ appropriate tone for this audience

_____ makes listeners comfortable

_____ reinforces message

_____ good timing

Style

_____ triads

_____ rhetorical questions

_____ repetition

_____ parallel structure

_____ wordplay

Audiovisual aids

_____ appropriate

_____ attractive

_____ easy for everyone to see/read

_____ not too many

_____ no fumbling

_____ no technical glitches

_____ not too expensive

Handouts

_____ adequate supply

_____ well-designed

_____ summarize main points

_____ provide contacts for more information
_____ reinforce speaker's credentials

Voice

_____ volume
_____ emphasis
_____ rate of speaking (not too fast, not too slow)
_____ varied speed (slower to set a particular mood, or faster to create excitement)
_____ effective pauses
_____ no "fillers" ("um," "ah," "uh")
_____ clarity:
* no slurred contractions ("wu'nt" for "wouldn't,")
* no reversed sounds ("modren" for "modern")
* no omitted sounds ("lists")
* no added sounds ("acrost")

Body Language

_____ effective gestures to reinforce the message
_____ appropriate smiles
_____ good eye contact
_____ no fidgeting!

Friendliness

_____ uses the word "you" to build rapport
_____ includes many personal pronouns ("we," "I," "our" ...)
_____ sincerely addresses audience's needs
_____ conversational
_____ good energy level
_____ appropriate smile

Q&A Session

_____ seems well-prepared

_____ gives solid answers

_____ volunteers to provide extra information for those who would like it

_____ fosters networking

_____ offers strong wrap-up

Build on Your Strengths

Humorist Garrison Keillor once said, "After a show, you only think about what you did wrong."

Governor Mario Cuomo also made a similar observation. Cuomo admitted that he didn't always know when he had given a good speech, but he was usually able to identify the bad ones.

That's true with most speakers. We have an amazing ability to zero in on our weaknesses. And that's good, because we learn from our mistakes. But we also learn from our strengths. So it's smart to identify the things we already do well.

The next time you walk away from a big speech or an important phone call or a difficult meeting, give yourself credit for the things you said right:

THINGS I SAID RIGHT

(1) _____

(2) _____

(3) _____

(4) _____

(5) _____

Identify People Who Can Help You Improve as a Speaker

You'll become more successful as a speaker if you have good people you can turn to for help. Start by identifying all the people you already know who can give you support in improving your communications skills.

"I know at least one person who can . . ."

_____ ". . . provide good research."

_____ ". . . produce great slides."

_____ ". . . edit my speech manuscript."

_____ ". . . proofread my handouts."

_____ ". . . critique my rehearsals."

_____ ". . . help me practice for the Q&A session."

_____ ". . . meet periodically to form a speaker support group."

_____ ". . . prepare the room." (Check the sound, fix the seating, adjust the lights, et cetera.)

_____ ". . . attend the presentation to make notes on my delivery."

_____ ". . . tape-record or videotape my speeches." (So I can "critique" myself later on.)

_____ ". . . distribute handouts."

_____ ". . . manage an on-site 'information table.' "

If you don't already know people who can help you, get busy and find some. Ideally, you will want at least one person who can help in each category. If you're lucky, you will have colleagues, friends, and relatives who can help in several areas. Be very nice to these people.

Measuring Your Effectiveness

"You can see a lot by observing."
—YOGI BERRA

"WAS MY SPEECH A SUCCESS?"

The more you can answer "yes," the greater your success.

	YES	NO

What happened during the speech?
    (1) Did the audience applaud when I was introduced? _____ _____
    (2) Did the audience look interested? _____ _____
    (3) Did they nod their heads in agreement? _____ _____
    (4) Did the audience stay the whole time? _____ _____
    (5) Did I get more applause than the other speakers? _____ _____
    (6) Did the audience smile and make strong eye contact? _____ _____
    (7) Did they laugh at appropriate spots? _____ _____

What happened after the speech?
    (8) Did the audience ask good questions? _____ _____
    (9) Were my handouts taken (and not left on seats)? _____ _____

	YES	NO
(10) Did people request copies of my slides?	_____	_____
(11) Did they ask for audiotapes, or written transcripts?	_____	_____
(12) Did people request business cards or promotional material?	_____	_____
(13) Did they take notes and ask for additional information?	_____	_____
(14) Did they send complimentary letters or make phone calls?	_____	_____
(15) Was I immediately invited back to speak next year?	_____	_____
(16) Did I receive invitations to speak at other events?	_____	_____
(17) Did reporters call for interviews?	_____	_____
(18) Were the evaluation forms positive?	_____	_____
(19) Did my public *actions* reinforce my *message*?	_____	_____

(NOTE: Nothing will undercut your speaking credibility more than saying one thing during a speech . . . and then later doing something else. Make sure your public actions reinforce your public words.)

Get an Audience Evaluation

No matter how sincerely you try to evaluate your own presentations, you need "the ultimate evaluation" . . . and that can come only from your audience. Try to get audience feedback on every major presentation. Keep your evaluations short. Audiences simply won't fill out a form if it takes too long.

TIP: If you limit the number of fill-in-the-blank questions, you'll get an even greater response. Audiences prefer yes/no statements or multiple-choice questions because they're easier (and faster) to answer.

A simple marketing suggestion: Be sure to offer at least one place where audiences can write (in their own words) what they most liked about your speech. Aside from giving you insight into the most popular parts of your presentation, these recommendations can later be used as testimonials.

EVALUATION FORM:

[Name of Speaker]

Please evaluate the speaker using this rating scale:

 5 = excellent; 4 = very good; 3 = good; 2 = fair; 1 = poor

    topic _____
    content _____
    delivery _____
    handouts _____
    audiovisual _____
    facilities _____
    Q&A session _____

Would you recommend this speaker to other groups?

[ ] yes [ ] no

What did you like best about this speaker? _____

_____

_____

If you would like to know about future programs, please give your name/address:

               _____

               _____

               _____

               _____

Thanks for your feedback.

Learning from Other Speakers

*"You must learn from the mistakes of others.
You can't possibly live long enough to make them
all yourself."*
—SAM LEVENSON, HUMORIST

Think of it this way, if you want to improve your French, you'll join a French conversation group. The same holds true for public speaking. If you want to keep improving your speaking skills, you need to connect with others who share your commitment to good communication.

I often recommend Toastmasters as an excellent starting place to improve your speaking skills. (You can learn more about the benefits of this organization in the appendix in Section Eight.) But you can also form your own "self-help" groups. Focus on people who might be willing to meet periodically in a "speaker support group."

"HELPING EACH OTHER"

A group exercise to improve speaking skills.
(Total: 45 minutes)

Step One: Select
Choose a group of four people who have comparable speaking skills.

Step Two: Tell

Take five minutes to describe your most recent speaking experience to the group. Share specific details about *what worked* and *what didn't work*. Then take turns, allowing everyone to describe their own experiences for five minutes *without interruption*. Use a timer so each person stays on track.

Step Three: Listen

Encourage active listening throughout the exercise. Hold comments until everyone has had a chance to describe their speaking experience.

Step Four: Help

Encourage group discussion. Allow five minutes to address *each* person's speaking situation—offering practical suggestions for future improvement.

Learning from a Professional Coach

You can do a lot to help yourself by following the guidelines in this book. You can also improve by learning from other speakers in various support groups. But if you want to give your presentations the professional advantage, then consider hiring a skilled speech coach.

An experienced coach will readily identify your strengths and weaknesses—and plan a custom-designed consulting session that's targeted to your unique speaking needs. You will become a better presenter . . . and save tremendous time in the process.

WHEN SHOULD YOU HIRE A PROFESSIONAL SPEECH COACH?

- When it's especially important for you to do a terrific job
- When you're speaking to an influential audience
- When the media might be in attendance
- When dynamic speaking skills could boost your career (or when *weak* presentation skills could *harm* your career)
- When you need to save time (An experienced speech coach can dramatically shorten your preparation time. Why spend weeks spinning your wheels on a big speech when a professional can streamline the entire process?)
- When you want to see immediate results (One or two sessions with a skilled coach will yield excellent results.)
- When confidentiality is important (Must you give a presentation that deals with sensitive information? This is not appropriate for group rehearsals.)
- When you must tackle embarrassing delivery flaws (Are you embarrassed about your voice? Is your body language awkward? You probably don't want to address these private problems in a public course—but if you don't address your problems, you'll never fix them. Individual attention from a professional coach would prove beneficial.)

WHAT QUESTIONS SHOULD YOU ASK WHEN HIRING A SPEECH COACH?

"What is your fee?" is the obvious question. But, don't start there. Ask the more important questions first.

- "Who will do the actual coaching?" Many firms sub-contract—meaning, if "Coach A" isn't available, they will send "Coach B." Don't get stuck with an inexperienced assistant or a last-minute substitute.
- "How long have you been coaching speakers?" You want someone with experience . . . someone who can help you deal with virtually any speaking situation.
- "Are presentation skills your specialty?" You don't want a trainer who teaches "Public Speaking 101" on Monday, "Time Management Skills" on Tuesday, and "Business Etiquette" on Wednesday.
- "What have you published in the field?" Ask to read any magazine articles they might have written. This is an excellent way to see how they approach their craft.
- "Who are some of your recent/current clients?" While confidentiality is always an issue, a professional speech coach should be able to give you the names of reputable clients as references.
- "Do you have long-standing relationships with your clients?" If Client X hires the same speech coach every year for the annual sales meeting, you can be sure Client X is pleased with the results.
- "What professional organizations are you active in?" Certain organizations hold members to higher ethical standards. It always helps to know about your consultant's memberships.

- "Can you offer constructive criticism?" If you want to improve your speaking skills, you will need to make some changes in your delivery. This is not the time to hire a "head-nodder." Instead, you need a coach who's honest enough to identify your problem areas.
- "Will you make yourself available to answer my questions after our session is over?" Let's say you worked with a speech coach a month ago and made good progress. But now you find yourself facing a last-minute presentation—and, frankly, you could use a little help. Can you call or e-mail your speech coach for some guidance and encouragement?

Only now do you have enough information to ask intelligent questions about fees. Ask, "What is your basic fee structure?"—and then get specifics.

- "How would your fee change for multiple bookings?" Many coaches will charge a lower day rate if you book several days at a time.
- "What would it cost to train additional participants?" If a coach quotes you a fee for training three executives in a day, how much more would it cost to add another executive to that training session?
- "What travel costs will you incur?" You have a right to expect an estimate in advance. And you have the right to insist that all travel be kept *reasonable*. Do not accept any surprises about First Class airline tickets or luxury hotel suites.
- "Does your fee include any books?" Ask if the books can be autographed. Participants see this as an "added value"—and most authors are delighted to oblige.

- "What handouts will be provided?" Be clear about who will handle the photocopying of all these materials. CAUTION: Copyrighted materials may *not* be photocopied without the written permission of the copyright holder. If you hire a consultant to train ten executives, you may not copy the handouts to train others in your organization.

Appendix
Useful Books, Websites, and Professional Organizations

Useful Books

ANECDOTES—GENERAL

Hodgin, Michael. *1001 More Humorous Illustrations for Public Speaking*. Grand Rapids, Michigan: Zondervan Publishing House, 1998.
A wide variety of ancedotes—ranging from sports to church issues. Good material for general speakers as well as pastors. Excellent index of subtopics, index of titles, and list of sources.

Fadiman, Clifton. *The Little, Brown Book of Anecdotes*. New York: Little, Brown, 1985.
There are newer books, but none better. This book will always hold a prime spot on my bookshelf. It offers more than 4,000 well-researched anecdotes about 2,000 famous people—from Alexander Graham Bell to Frank Lloyd Wright. Valuable subject index, source list, and bibliography. You can count on this book for excellent material.

Van Ekeren, Glenn. *The Speaker's Sourcebook II*. Englewood Cliffs, New Jersey: Prentice-Hall, 1994.

A wide range of motivational material covering 75 topics. You'll find Carl Sagan on "Imagination," Mother Teresa on "Adversity," and Buck Rogers on "Motivation." Index.

BIRTHDAY CELEBRATIONS

Morris, Desmond. *The Book of Ages*. New York: Penguin, 1983.

This book has been around a long while, but it's still a terrific source if you want to say a few clever words at someone's birthday party.

* *Age fifty*: "For certain people, after fifty, litigation takes the place of sex." (Gore Vidal)
* *Age sixty-five*: "I'm sixty-five and I guess that puts me in with the geriatrics, but if there were fifteen months in every year, I'd only be forty-eight." (James Thurber)
* *Age seventy-five*: "I am ready to meet my Maker. Whether my Maker is prepared for the ordeal of meeting me is another matter." (Winston Churchill)

Sampson, Anthony and Sally. *The Oxford Book of Ages*. New York: Oxford University Press, 1988.

Quotations and poetry about every year of life—from the age of one to one hundred.

* "At twenty years of age, the will reigns; at thirty, the wit; and at forty, the judgement." (Benjamin Franklin)
* "One starts to get young at the age of sixty, and then it's too late." (Picasso)
* "The years between fifty and seventy are the hardest. You are always being asked to do things, and yet you are not decrepit enough to turn them down." (T. S. Eliot)

BUSINESS-RELATED QUOTATIONS

Boone, Louis E. *Quotable Business*. New York: Random House, 1992.

Over 2,800 funny, irreverent, and insightful quotations about corporate life, including:

* *accounting*: "Specialists in finance must be on tap, but they should never be on top." (Al Newharth)
* *strategy*: "In baiting a mouse trap with cheese, always leave room for the mouse." (Saki)

Eigen, Lewish, and Jonathan Siegel. *The Manager's Book of Quotations*. New York: AMACOM, 1989.

Well-researched quotations covering 47 topics, including:

* *rules, red tape, and bureaucracy*: "We can overcome gravity, but sometimes the paperwork is overwhelming. (Werhner Von Braun, pioneer rocket scientist)
* *strategic thinking*: "There is no security on this earth; there is only opportunity." (Douglas MacArthur)
* *team building*: "No star playing, just football." (Knute Rockne, coach, Notre Dame University football team)

Griffith, Joe. *Speaker's Library of Business Stories, Anecdotes, and Humor*. Englewood Cliffs, New Jersey: Prentice-Hall, 1990.

A lively collection covering 200 managerial topics (training, entrepreneurship, ethics, etc.). Get great "inside" stories from companies such as Disney, Domino's Pizza, Sears, and Chrysler.

Hay, Peter. *The Book of Business Anecdotes*. New York: Facts on File, 1988.

Conveniently organized by subject—from "Money," to "Selling," to "Corporate Culture." Outstanding bibliography, helpful index.

Calendar/Daily Listings

Dickson, Paul. *Timelines: Day by Day and Trend by Trend from the Dawn of the Atomic Age to the Gulf War.* Reading, Massachusetts: Addison Wesley Publishing, 1991.

This is the best book of its kind. Suppose your organization was founded in 1961, and you want to find interesting details about that year. This book offers great tidbits that can make any presentation more interesting. In 1961, for example,

* Hoffman-Laroche introduced Valium.
* *Webster's Third New International Dictionary* set off debates by including *ain't* for the first time.
* the White House began a big push for physical fitness.
* the Peace Corps attracted many idealistic young people.

Mason, Eileen. *Witty Words*. New York: Sterling Publishing, 1992.

An excellent way to find out what happened in history on May 17 or August 12, or whenever you happen to be speaking. You'll get great quips for Stockbroker's Day, National Aviation Day, Transportation Week, and many others. Delightful material.

Definitions

Brussell, Eugene E. *Webster's New World Dictionary of Quotable Definitions.* Englewood Cliffs, New Jersey: Prentice-Hall, 1988.

This book is worth its weight in gold for any speaker. Need a clever definition for an upcoming talk? Forget your regular dictionary. Instead, turn to this book for more than 17,000 lively definitions on 2,000 subjects.

* *inflation*: "Too much money going to somebody else." (William Vaughan)

* *decision*: "What a man makes when he can't find anybody to serve on a committee."(Fletcher Knebel)
* *telephone*: "The greatest nuisance among the conveniences, the greatest convenience among the nuisances." (Robert Lynd)
* *television*: "Chewing gum for the eyes." (John Mason Brown)

EDUCATION

Bronner, Simon J. *Piled Higher and Deeper: The Folklore of Campus Life*. Little Rock, Arkansas: August House Publishers, 1990.

Giving a commencement address or a homecoming toast? Turn here. You'll find well-researched folklore dealing with campus issues like final exams, absentminded professors, fraternity pledging, and faculty quirks. Where else could you learn about:

* Notre Dame's bizarre animal race?
* Baylor University's celebration of Sam Houston?
* Spalding University's annual Running of the Rodents?

ENVIRONMENTAL QUOTATIONS

Rodes, Barbara K., and Odell Rice. *A Dictionary of Environmental Quotations*. Baltimore, Maryland: The Johns Hopkins University Press, 1992.

One of the few places to find good quotations about the environment.

* "This planet is not private property." (Hazel Henderson)
* "If people destroy something replaceable made by mankind, they are called vandals; If they destroy some-

thing irreplaceable made by God, they are called developers." (Joseph Word Krutch)

ETHNIC/REGIONAL

De Ley, Gerd. *African Proverbs*. New York: Hippocrene Books, 1999.
    An excellent volume, offering material that isn't easily found elsewhere. Very well organized. It identifies proverbs by country, by province, and even by tribe. Provides photos, a helpful bibliography, and an appendix with information on various tribes.

De Ley, Gerd. *International Dictionary of Proverbs*. New York: Hippocrene Books, 1998.
    An indispensable book for any international speaker. Preparing for a conference in Austria or a meeting in Chile? This unique book can help. You'll find 8,000 proverbs organized by country or region—from the Balearic Isles and Croatia, to Togo and the Ukraine. It offers a particularly strong section on Yiddish proverbs.

Hanki, Joseph. *Arabic Proverbs*. New York: Hippocrene Books, 1998.
    Provides side-by-side English translations of hard-to-find materials.

Jones, Loyal, and Billy Edd Wheeler. *Laughter in Appalalchia: A Festival of Southern Mountain Humor*. Little Rock, Arkansas: August House Publishers, 1987.
    Anecdotes about "Doctors and Lawyers," "Schools," "Religion," and "Politics." [NOTE: August House prides itself on an outstanding American Folklore Series, representing about a dozen cultures. For a catalog, visit www.augusthouse.com, or

contact August House Publishers, Inc., P.O. Box 3223, Little Rock, Arkansas 72203.]

O'Farrell, Padraic. *Irish Toasts, Curses and Blessings*. New York: Sterling, 1995.
   Absolutely wonderful entries. My favorite:

   * "May you never see a bad day—and if it sees you, may it be wearing glasses."

Sherman, Josepha. *A Sampler of Jewish American Folklore*. Little Rock, Arkansas: August House Publishers, 1992.
   Wit and wisdom from the Old World to the New. Some chapters deal with ceremonial topics (birth, marriage, death). Other chapters provide humorous stories, proverbs, riddles, and clever folk tales. Especially helpful: detailed notes and a bibliography.

Telushkin, Joseph. *Uncommon Wisdom*. New York: Shapolsky Publishers, 1987.
   This book offers seldom-seen Talmudic blessings, biblical stories, and rabbinical observations. It also has wonderful quips from popular contemporary sources. It's divided into sections based on the traditional categories of Jewish commandments: "Between Man and Man" and "Between Man and God."

   * "I don't want to achieve immortality through my work. I want to achieve it through not dying." (Woody Allen)
   * "Too bad that all the people who know how to run the country are busy driving taxicabs and cutting hair." (George Burns)

Weinrich, Beatrice Silverman. *Yiddish Folktales*. New York: Pantheon Books, 1988.

Almost 200 marvelous tales from the world of Eastern European Jewry. These stories are all rich in custom, history, wit, and imagination. [SPECIAL NOTE: The Pantheon Fairy Tale and Folklore Library also publishes great collections of folklore from Africa, Japan, Ireland, and elsewhere.]

West, John O. *Mexican-American Folklore*. Little Rock, Arkansas: August House Publishers, 1988.

Legends, songs, proverbs, tales of saints, stories of revolutionaries, and much more.

EULOGIES

McNees, Pat, ed. *Dying: A Book of Comfort*. New York: Warner Books, 1998.

A superb collection of quotations, literary passages and prayers about the subject of death. Many of the selections are appropriate for reading at funerals and memorial services—expressing your thoughts and feelings at a time when you may be at a loss for words. This is a valuable resource for anyone of any faith who must deliver a eulogy.

FOOD

Cader, Michael, with Debby Roth. *Eat These Words*. New York: HarperCollins, 1991.

A tiny book, filled with great fun. Where else could you find the following:

* "Sex is good, but not as good as fresh sweet corn." (Garrison Keillor)
* "In England, there are sixty different religions, but only one sauce." (Voltaire)

Egerton, March, ed. *Since Eve Ate Apples*. Portland, Oregon: Tsunami Press, 1994.

An outstanding reference book for anyone who cares about dining. Well-organized, with 161 categories arranged alphabetically, and all quotations presented chronologically. Excellent source notations.

* "Exercise is a modern superstition, invented by people who ate too much, and had nothing to think about." (George Santayana)
* "Security is a smile from a headwaiter." (Russell Baker)

HISTORY

Frost, Elizabeth. *The Bully Pulpit*. New York: Facts on File, 1988.

If you want presidential quotes, go here first. This is your best source.

Mencken, H. L. *A New Dictionary of Quotations*. New York: Knopf, 1987.

A truly excellent volume. Superbly researched, carefully annotated, and well-organized. In spite of the huge size, you can find things easily. This reference work is especially valuable for providing the thoughts of significant figures in history and literature, including Thomas Carlyle, Karl Marx, Thomas Paine, and Oliver Wendell Holmes.

HUMOR

Blumenfeld, Esther, and Lynne Alpern. *The Smile Connection: How to Use Humor in Dealing with People*. Englewood Cliffs, New Jersey: Prentice-Hall, 1986.

A helpful guide, filled with examples and funny lines for everyday use.

Jones, Loyal, and Billy Edd Wheeler. *Hometown Humor, U.S.A.* Little Rock, Arkansas: August House Publishers, 1991.
    Country humor on a wide range of topics: "Aging," "Health," "Farmers," "Education," "Law," "Politics," "Preachers," and "City Folks."

Metcalf, Fred. *The Penguin Dictionary of Modern Humorous Quotations.* London: Penguin, 1986.
    This is a wonderful book—useful for speakers and writers, and downright fun for browsers. Offers a decidedly British bent; strong with European references.

* *anxiety*: "I have a new philosophy. I'm only going to dread one day at a time." (Charles Schultz, from a *Peanuts* cartoon)
* *church*: "Go to church this Sunday—avoid the Christmas rush." (graffiti)
* *Europe*: "European Community institutions have produced European beets, butter, cheese, wine, veal, and even pigs. But they have not produced Europeans." (Louise Weiss)
* *London*: "When it's three o'clock in New York, it's still 1938 in London." (Bette Midler)
* *work*: "Work is much more fun than fun." (Noël Coward)

Pentz, Croft M. *The Complete Book of Zingers.* Wheaton, Illinois: Tyndale House Publishers, 1990.
    The author is an Assemblies of God minister who set out to compile a witty collection of "one-sentence sermons." He succeeded. A wide range of topics, including:

* *work*: "Pray to God, but row for shore."
* *illness*: "Virus is a Latin word used by doctors to mean, 'Your guess is as good as mine.'"
* *determination*: "Trying times are no time to quit trying."

Perret, Gene, and Linda Perret. *Funny Business*. Englewood Cliffs, New Jersey: Prentice-Hall, 1990.

An indispensable book, with terrific one-liners that cover just about everything in the business world. It even has a funny section of quips on "Office Air-Conditioning." Now, what more could any business speaker ask for? Includes the following topics:

* Cheap Bosses
* Advertising
* Seminars
* Office Collections
* Personnel
* Résumés
* Mandatory Retirement
* Executive Perks
* Memo Writing
* Job Application Forms

Rees, Nigel. *Cassel Dictionary of Humorous Quotations*. New York: Sterling Publishing, 1998.

Great quips about:

* *lawmaking*: "If you like laws and sausages, you should never watch either one being made."
* *saving*: "Saving is a very fine thing, especially when your parents have done it for you." (Winston Churchill)
* *schedule*: "There cannot be a crisis next week. My schedule is already full." (Henry Kissinger)

MILITARY

Charlton, James. *The Military Quotation Book*. New York: St. Martin's Press, 1990.
  Great lines—witty, pithy, short. No subject index.

  * "War is too important to be left to the generals." (Georges Clemençeau)
  * "One man with courage makes a majority." (Andrew Jackson)
  * "The mere absence of war is not peace." (John F. Kennedy)
  * "In war, there is no second prize for the runner up." (General Omar Bradley)

POLITICS/GOVERNMENT

Baker, Daniel B. *Power Quotes*. Detroit: Gale Research, 1992.
  You'll find 4,000 trenchant sound bites about every aspect of politics and government. Well-researched, with outstanding source information.

Henning, Charles. *The Wit and Wisdom of Politics*. Golden, Colorado: Fulcrum, 1989.
  While focusing on politics, this book also includes great quotes about a wide range of related subjects:

  * *lawyers*: "It is the trade of lawyers to question everything, yield nothing, and to talk by the hour." (Thomas Jefferson)
  * *debt*: "Blessed are the young, for they shall inherit the national debt." (Herbert Hoover)

* *voting*: "Whenever a fellow tells me he is bipartisan, I know he's going to vote against me." (Harry S. Truman)

PROVERBS

Auden, W. H., and Louis Kronenberger. *The Viking Book of Aphorisms*. New York: Penguin Books, 1966.

Several decades old . . . and still one of the best reference sources available. More than 3,000 wise and witty comments.

Fergusson, Rosalind. *The Penguin Dictionary of Proverbs*. New York: Penguin Books, 1983.

Handy arrangement, easy-to-use chapters.

QUOTATIONS—GENERAL

Allen, Jessica. *Quotable Men of the Twentieth Century*. New York: William Morrow and Company, 1999.

Covers a wide range of contemporary topics, from bureaucracy to divorce to technology.

Camp, Wesley D. *What a Piece of Work Is Man!* Englewood Cliffs, New Jersey: Prentice-Hall, 1990.

An outstanding collection of hard-to-find quotations from 2000 B.C. to the present. Well-organized and well-documented. A phenomenal range of topics, offering refreshingly unfamiliar quotations:

* *circumstances*: "Man is not the creature of circumstances. Circumstances are the creatures of men." (Benjamin Disraeli)
* *civilization*: ". . . a movement and not a condition, a voyage and not a harbor." (Arnold Toynbee)

* *loss*: "You must lose a fly to catch a trout." (George Herbert)
* *retirement*: "I married him for better or for worse, but not for lunch." (Hazel Weiss, after her husband retired as general manager of the Yankees)
* *translating*: "The art of translating lies less in knowing the other language than in knowing your own." (Ned Rorem)

Cook, John. *The Book of Positive Quotations*. Minneapolis: Fairview Press, 1993.

Ideal for motivational speeches. Very well organized, so it's easy to find what you want (for example, the chapter of "Acceptance" has 18 sections, allowing you to target your material quickly). Divided into these six parts:

* Peace of Mind
* Living One Day at a Time
* Preparing for Success
* Knowing What to Do
* Overcoming Negativism and Uncertainties
* Making Dreams Come True

Ehrlich, Eugene, and Marshall deBruhl. *The International Thesaurus of Quotations*. New York: HarperCollins, 1996

A truly comprehensive research tool. Over 16,000 entries, spanning 2,500 years, covering 1,000 subject categories. Offers an outstanding index of authors, an index of key words, and an index of categories.

* *retirement*: "Cessation of work, not accompanied by cessation of expenses." (Cato the Elder, second century B.C.)

Frank, Leonard Roy, ed. *Random House Webster's Quotationary*. New York: Random House, 1999.

A remarkable collection, with over 20,000 entries on a wide range of topics:

* *change*: "It is a secret, both in nature and state, that it is safer to change many things than one." (Francis Bacon)
* *failure*: "In life as in football, fall forward when you fall." (Arthur Guitterman)
* *leadership*: "A genuine leader is not a searcher for consensus but a molder of consensus." (Dr. Martin Luther King Jr.)

Gaither, C. C., and A. E. Cavozov-Gaither. *Statistically Speaking*. Philadelphia: Institute of Physics Publishing, 1996.

The most comprehensive collection of quotations pertaining to statistics. An extraordinary reference work—with detailed bibliography and indexes. A surprisingly wide range of chapters, including:

* Cause and Effect
* Predictions
* Quality Control
* Chance
* Graphics

Marsden, C. R. S. *Dictionary of Outrageous Quotations*. Topsfield, Massachusetts: Salem House, 1988.

This is not a "basic" reference book. But if you're looking for quirky comments, flip one-liners, and irreverent messages . . . well, you can find them in here.

Platt, Suzy, ed. *Respectfully Quoted*. New York: Barnes and Noble Books, 1993.

A wealth of classical and modern quotations, international in scope. Conveniently indexed by subject, author, and keyword. Backed by solid research, it offers helpful historical notes for each quotation.

Rawson, Hugh. *Unwritten Laws: The Unofficial Rules of Life*. New York: Crown, 1998.
Catchy slogans and one-liners.

* "Nine-tenths of wisdom consists in being wise in time." (Theodore Roosevelt)
* "Money isn't everything as long as you have enough." (Malcolm Forbes)

Rees, Nigel. *Brewer's Quotations: A Phrase and Fable Dictionary*. New York: Sterling Publishing, 1995.
This wonderful book contains "the most commonly misquoted, misattributed, misascribed, misremembered and most disputed sayings that there are"—and puts them in their proper historical context. An outstanding index.

Shanahan, John M., ed. *The Most Brilliant Thoughts of All Time*. New York: HarperCollins Publishers, 1999.
What makes this so great for speakers? The entries are very short (running two lines or less) so they'll fit easily into your message and sound conversational. Some favorites:

* "In the field of observation, chance favors the prepared mind." (Louis Pasteur)
* "You don't hold your own in the world by standing on guard, but by attacking and getting well hammered yourself." (George Bernard Shaw)

Simpson, James B., and Daniel J. Boorstin. *Simpson's Contemporary Quotations*. Boston: Houghton Mifflin, 1988.

Filled with 10,000 post-1950 quotes. Very easy to use—with a helpful table of contents, an index of sources, and an index of subjects and key lines. Plus you'll find separate chapters about different occupations (military officers, doctors, lawyers, reporters, entertainers, restaurateurs, you name it).

RELIGION/PHILOSOPHY

Cook, John. *Timeless Quotations on Faith and Belief.* Minneapolis: Fairview Press, 1997.

An outstanding variety of quotations on prayer, forgiveness, blessings, and other topics.

Freeman, Criswell. *The Book of Christmas Wisdom.* Nashville: Walnut Grove Press, 1999.

The best place to find words concerning this holiday.

* "Santa Claus comes under many names: Kris Kringle, Saint Nicholas, Mastercard . . ." (Phyllis Diller)
* "On this Christmas, may we, the people of every race, nation, and religion, learn to love one another and to forgive and be forgiven. Then the peace of Christ will prevail." (Coretta Scott King)

Peale, Dr. Norman Vincent. *My Favorite Quotations.* New York: Giniger, 1990.

The best-selling author of *The Power of Positive Thinking* shares his favorite quotes on a variety of subjects: relationships, enthusiasm, God's creation, mental health, pain, suffering, healing, community, aging.

Tomlinson, Gerald. *Treasury of Religious Quotations.* Englewood Cliffs, New Jersey: Prentice-Hall, 1991.

Organized into 149 topics (from "Achievement and Action" to "Sorrow and Values"), then subdivided into 30 religions and beliefs (with hard-to-find entries from Mormonism and Islam). As an example, the "Leadership" category includes:

* *Christianity*: "Can the blind lead the blind? Shall they not both fall into the ditch?" (Holy Bible, Luke: 6:39)
* *Judaism*: "In the place where there is already a leader, do not seek to become a leader. But in the place where there is no leader, strive thou to become a leader." (Talmud, Berakot 63a)

Well, Albert M., Jr. *Inspiring Quotations*. Nashville: Thomas Nelson, 1988.

More than 3,000 quotes from leading evangelicals, poets, philosophers, etc. This reference book places a strong emphasis on fundamental Christian concerns—with chapters ranging from "Abortion and Atheism" to "World Peace and Worship."

Winokur, Jon. *Zen to Go*. New York: New American Library, 1989.

Sound bites of wisdom from an astonishing cross-section of thinkers—from the Buddha and Lao Tzu to Jack Kerouac and Kurt Vonnegut Jr. Any book that can cite comedian George Carlin in the same breath as Goethe and Dag Hammarskjöld gets my attention.

* "There are children playing in the street who could solve some of my top problems in physics, because they have modes of sensory perception that I lost long ago." (J. Robert Oppenheimer)
* "Computers are useless. They can only give you answers." (Pablo Picasso)

* "When you're green, you're growing. When you're ripe, you rot." (Ray Kroc)

SPEECH MANUSCRIPTS

Safire, William. *Lend Me Your Ears: Great Speeches in History*. New York: W. W. Norton & Company, 1992.

An outstanding collection of:

* Memorials and Patriotic Speeches
* War and Revolution Speeches
* Tributes and Eulogies
* Debates and Argumentation
* Trials
* Gallows and Farewell Speeches
* Sermons
* Inspirational Speeches
* Lectures and Instructive Speeches
* Speeches of Social Responsibility
* Media Speeches
* Political Speeches
* Commencement Speeches

SPORTS

Tomlinson, Gerald, ed. *Speaker's Treasury of Sports Anecdotes, Stories, and Humor*. Englewood Cliffs, New Jersey: Prentice-Hall, 1990.

Divided into seventy-two categories, covering fifty-four different sports and activities. It also offers a day-by-day sports calendar, as well as birthday listings for sports stars.

STORYTELLING

Lipman, Doug. *The Storytelling Coach*. Little Rock, Arkansas: August House Publishers, 1995.

Helpful principles and motivational advice for communicating your stories—in the classroom, in the boardroom, from the pulpit, from the stage.

Mooney, Bill, and David Holt. *The Storyteller's Guide*. Little Rock, Arkansas: August House Publishers, 1996.

Packed with well-chosen anecdotes, examples, and parables that illuminate the art of storytelling. Features interviews with more than fifty experienced storytellers—including teachers, librarians, authors, actors, and clergymen.

TOASTS/ROASTS/SPECIAL OCCASIONS

Detz, Joan. *Can You Say a Few Words?* New York: St. Martin's Press, 1991.

Practical speaking advice for special occasions, including:

* award ceremonies
* retirements
* acceptance speeches
* sports banquets
* patriotic ceremonies
* anniversary tributes
* commencements
* eulogies

Diagram Group. *The Little Giant Encyclopedia of Toasts and Quotes*. New York: Sterling Publishing, 1998.

Roasts for all occasions. Toasts for weddings, anniversaries, graduations, retirements.

Evans, William R., III, and Andrew Frothingham. *Crisp Toasts.* New York: St. Martin's Press, 1992.

Covers a wide range of topics (from "Charity" to "Prosperity") and gives one-liners for many professions. Also gives quips for popular events (from New Year's to christenings to anniversaries).

McManus, Ed, and Bill Nicholas. *We're Roasting Harry Tuesday Night.* Englewood Cliffs, New Jersey: Prentice-Hall, 1988.

How to plan, write, and conduct the business/social roast. Also offers ready-to-use lines, such as:

* "Harry was a consultant. That's a guy who quit work, but kept the breaks and lunch."
* "It's not easy writing speeches for Harry: you are limited to words and concepts that he understands."
* "Harry doesn't personally have ulcers, but he is a carrier."

Pasta, Elmer. *Complete Books of Roasts, Boasts and Toasts.* West Nyack, New York: Parker Publishing, 1982.

This book has quips for every occupation imaginable:

* budget planner
* broadcasting executive
* forester
* podiatrist
* stuntperson
* surgeon
* ticket taker
* traffic manager

WEATHER

Freier, George D., Ph.D. *Weather Proverbs*. Tucson, Arizona: Fisher Books, 1989.

Giving a presentation the same day as a blizzard? Did the audience have to drive through pouring rain to attend? This book can give you some clever tie-ins.

WOMEN

Maggio, Rosalie. *Quotations by Women*. Boston: Beacon Press, 1996.

Offers 16,000 quotations, covering an extraordinary range of subjects. An outstanding index of subjects and key lines. Well-researched, with excellent source material. My favorites:

* "Democracy is not a spectator sport." (Marian Wright Edelman)
* "Cats think about three things: food, sex, and nothing." (Adair Lara)
* "I don't waste time thinking, 'Am I doing it right?' I say, 'Am I doing it?' " (Georgette Mosbacher)
* "Suffering makes you deep. Travel makes you broad. In case I get my pick, I'd rather travel." (Judith Viorst)

Warner, Carolyn. *The Last Word*. Englewood Cliffs, New Jersey: Prentice-Hall, 1992.

Covers women's voices from all fields—from Eleanor Roosevelt and Pearl Buck to Mary Kay Ash and Erma Bombeck. It even offers this wise tidbit from Miss Piggy: "Never eat more than you can lift." (Indeed.)

Useful Professional Organizations

American Library Association, 50 East Huron Street, Chicago, IL, 60611; (800) 545-2433. Fax on demand: (800) 545-2433, press #4.

International Association of Business Communicators, One Hallidie Plaza, Suite 600, San Francisco, CA, 94102; (415) 433-3400.

National Storytelling Network, 116½ West Main St., Jonesborough, TN, 37659; (800) 525-4514.

Public Relations Society of America, 33 Irving Place, New York, NY, 10003; (212) 995-2230.

Toastmasters International, 23182 Arroyo Vista, Rancho Santa Margarita, CA, 92688–2620; (949) 858-8255; (800) 9WE-SPEAK [toll free phone number for a free listing of local clubs]; www.toastmasters.org.

This is the world's largest organization devoted to communication excellence. Your local Toastmasters Club will give you the chance to learn effective presentation skills through practical experience. The atmosphere is friendly and helpful, and the fees are very modest. An excellent starting point for anyone who wants to learn the best way to "say something."

Useful Websites for Speakers

Aphorisms, Proverbs, and Quotations

- * www.aphorismsgalore.com
- * www.columbia.edu/acis/bartleby/bartlett (*Bartlett's Familiar Quotations*)

BIOGRAPHICAL INFORMATION

* www.s9.com (This biographical dictionary can be searched by birth years, death years, titles, professions, literary/artistic works, and key achievements.)

DATE IN HISTORY

* http://dmarie.com/asp/history.asp?action=process (Fun for birthdays and anniversaries. Enter a date, and get newspaper headlines, sports stories, pop songs, and assorted trivia.)
* www.idea-bank.com (A well researched and well organized online database of quotations, humor and anecdotes—with a particularly good "History Today" file that offers material for each day of the year. Fee-based.)

DICTIONARIES

* www.onelook.com (An outstanding collection of dictionaries and glossaries.)

FAMOUS SPEECHES

* www.historyplace.com/speeches/previous.htm (Offers a wide assortment of speech texts, from St. Francis of Assisi's "Sermon to the Birds" to Lou Gehrig's "Farewell to Yankee Fans.")
* www.historychannel.com/gsspeech/archive.html (Features audio playbacks of "the words that changed the world." Includes presidential speeches.)
* www.winstonchurchill.org (The speeches of Winston Churchill.)

Index to the Internet

* www.lii.org (This librarians index to the Internet is particularly valuable. Just plug in a search term, and it brings up excellent sites.)

Newspapers Around the World

* www.thepaperboy.com
* www.ecola.com

Speechwriting and Presentation Skills

* www.joandetz.com (Articles about public speaking, tips for presentations, and seminar information.)

Song Titles

* www.lyrics.ch

U.S. History

* www.law.ou.edu/hist/ (The University of Oklahoma Law Center: A Chronology of U.S. Documents. Includes historical speeches and political documents—from the pre-Colonial era to the present.)

And now *you* get a chance to tell me how *you* say it. If you have any presentation tips you would like to share, or if you have any thoughts about this book, please let me know. E-mail me at jdetz@joandetz.com—or visit www.joandetz.com.

My best wishes for saying whatever you need to say in your own life!

INDEX